D1715451

The Exile's Papers

By the Same Author

Man in a Window, 1965 (Coach House Press)
Eighteen, 1966 (Coach House Press)
For Everyone, 1967 (Fleye Press)
Music for the Words, 1967 (privately printed)
The Machinery, 1967 (privately printed)
Alphabook, 1972 (Makework Press)
Glass/Passages, 1976 (Oberon Press)
An Ache in the Ear: 1966–1976, 1979 (Coach House Press)
Mirages, 1996 (privately printed)
On Abducting the 'Cello, 2004 (PQL)
The Book of Were, 2006 (PQL)
The Exile's Papers,
  Part One: The Duplicity of Autobiography, 2007 (PQL)
  Part Two: The Face As Its Thousand Ships, 2009 (PQL)
Jane Again, 2009 (Biblioasis)
Learning to Dance with a Peg Leg, 2009 (Frog Hollow Press)

Wayne Clifford
The Exile's Papers

THE DIRT'S PASSION IS FLESH SORROW

Part Three

The Porcupine's Quill

Library and Archives Canada Cataloguing in Publication

Clifford, Wayne, 1944–
    The exile's papers / Wayne Clifford.

Poems.
Pt. 2 published 2009 ; pt. 3 published 2011.
Contents: pt. 1. The duplicity of autobiography –
    pt. 2. The face as its thousand ships –
    pt. 3. The dirt's passion is flesh sorrow.
ISBN 978-0-88984-297-7 – ISBN 978-0-88984-317-2 (pt.2) –
ISBN 978-0-88984-344-8 (pt.3).

    I. Title.

PS8555.L535E94 2007   c811'.54   c2007-904140-x

1 2 3 4 • 13 12 11

Published by The Porcupine's Quill, Box 160, Erin, ON NOB 1TO.
http://porcupinesquill.ca

Represented in Canada by the Literary Press Group.
Trade orders are available from University of Toronto Press.

We acknowledge the support of the Ontario Arts Council and the Canada
Council for the Arts for our publishing program. The financial support of
the Government of Canada through the Canada Book Fund is also
gratefully acknowledged.

They're all used: the woman-form by wife;
the house design by this delighting house
but will be old, and moss come on its roof;
the dog-model by this pup arrived to bless
the old dog blanket with a living scent.
I've drunk the brook and pissed the brook, but brook
'sall falling seaward;
     all's
       what's been meant,
erased,
   rewritten in the pattern book.

Used, but not used up. The graves fill
with soil, the babes fill out with what the soil
heaps back. The smallest gods, in each small
life, unearth their clever tit for tat,
put their stakes down, win again the bet.

And cat space these years filled with Bastet.

Here, at the Now

I set out on a journey. Someone else
came back. And home seemed a mock-up elves
had glued from shattered memories set false
against a much too perfect background. Selves
of who had been a tourist, who had bought
the cheap, unpackable, bright, woven wares,
persisted, as did those of him who sought
at last an absolution from the cares
of things. Sunlight itself seemed thinned; the dark
was filled with shaky handholds, bed a grief
that brought a sleep with no relief, left stark
afterimages of deserts, and the too brief
comprehension he was somewhere else
at last, this stranger rousing in my pulse.

Dirt

Gran told me we eat a peck, but grit
puts most off, or whiff of rot. For the willing,
tones of apple, berry, sedge; the stiff
rudiments of sticks and stones that one,
at first, might expect to gag on;
                              grass,
timothy pulled stalk straight succulent.

Then subtleties, faint pretensions of what lives
collect, mostly unbragged, beyond the taint
of history's spilled blood, too much to cry
over:
          sweat of passions or labours, beery
piss, and such perfumes of our beastly
fashions as do deny the commonplace
dead, the bottom note, salt of earth.

Acquired, yes, but as a last meal, worth.

Empiricism **Is** *Imperium*

Worm uncoils in thawing soil
and begins again. If small April
rain down all darkens twilit
sap-sodden twigs, where no
shadow hinders humble progress,
worm's commerce opens dirt's
thin throats, and wrestles entrails
thru the clay, to cast those pasts
for telling, *I, worm, begin,*

so rouse to witness, first of shapes
the earth intimates, as present
as your most yearned caress,

in this expectant patch of lamp
exhume dark tailings of this pen.

Translated Heroship:
Urges from the Underworld

There was a couple, young, so that their bed …
ah, well, you know …
                        but she was bitten dead
by asp while running from the rapist, stuff
of prime TV, which never has enough.

A rock star, he, persuading even trees
to weep, whose style was strummed with air-harp ease
by g(r)eeks in towns so far and small,
                                 they knew,
did admen, he was *it!*, that one of few.

So sent him down to Hell to find his squeeze,
or,
    told him where to go,
                        and counted on
impulsiveness. Celebs respond to tease
like cats to nip. The urge gets bounded on.

This power struggle's many versions old.

But snares us still, its darkness has such hold.

Questioning's So Old, the Dog Cocked Her Head to a Raised Ending

But what's the shade enticed back up from Hell?
The world's weight of pennies on the lids
presses a swirled unvision. If dirt bids
forgetting in the dark –
                               but if tale must tell,
no matter the breath's clog, the choked cell,
a voice will find its way,
                               though dirt forbids
a mother tongue, a song, oration, rids
that voice of what in life had been said well.

Ha, Peter Sanger, clichés here to count!
Come count 'em, but I know a house whose well
is at the bottom of a graveyard's slope.
Such clear – so clean – each sip a fresh account.
Each sip as old as longing. Even Hell
relents that voice repeats deliquesced hope.

Two Voices out of the Background

Adam:

The angel spoke from noon's dazzle on sea,
and I heard nothing. The angel spoke from fire's
embers cinching, dying, the night closed.
I listened to the ash. I was afraid.
The angel spoke from the sway of my galloping heart,
but I didn't understand. The angel said,
'Stop!' The angel said, 'Here! Now!
'Your heart's a beast would carry me away!'

Then angel spoke, but I refused to hide.
I stood amidst a waste until green fell.
I breathed a cindered wind till blossom's scent.
Despite whatever bite of fruit might tell,
I knew the ache of rib and what it meant,
and was alone, until your warmth beside.

*

Lilith:

What first you told is that I slept in bone,
a left-side rib that sieved your blood through me
as marrow. So you took the right to own
my sex, my labour, and I'd never free,
you thought, myself from such a debt.

But I was ever dust, though I forgot
my birth, like any mortal. All you'll get
is what you give as equal. If my lot
is wife, then yours is husband, bound to wife
as surely as to season, seed and stock.

Your works and days must sum themselves as strife,
if you can't grasp that you mistook your cock
for sceptre. Sovereign from my inward out,
I reckon too the seeds, and how they sprout.

*

I've lasted as a name without her whole
retelling of the flesh, and of my want.
Oh, good enough a man, I would suppose,
whose soul could manifest as something role
could wring out then as history.
                            But just a cunt,
a bearer, sons as issue to your cause
and daughters throat-slit, set out in the sun,
on mountain....
                    Here's your other half, your whole
unguessed, the future so arrayed, you'd think
the world descended from your little dink.

I, *I*, am pod in which the seed is true.
I am the living vine. I'm the breath
out of ocean womb, and I'm the death
you must submit at last, as it comes due.

Adam:

You came of my left side's thirteenth rib.
I slept. And in my sleep I lay before
the Power of my making, clay Its ore.
From me It drew the rib to use as nib,
and traced your contours with Its breath as ink.

Now It must make again, since you have failed.
The rib from my right side will bring a mate
to comfort me, not prod my strength to hate.
Yes, rather daughters bled, than first sons killed,
to raise a needed wind, or let earth drink.

But though I let you go, I'll still make claim.
I own you by my spittle, by the stink
of my seed in your belly, and I'll blame
hereafter all my wrong on this cursed link.

*

Lilith:

If I had had a mother, you're the fool
she would have warned me of. Since you're fate's tool
and make just *things* yourself, by roughest rule
and much practice, you'll feel the nick as cruel
that none you make can ever have a soul.

Even if heaven's fire were power you stole,
nothing would come of it but the dead coal
you'd use to draw on cave wall. Of the world whole,
unparted through to mystery, you howl
your ignorance as your dog-slave does to foul
the night air for the flight of sacred owl.

You say you own me and expect I'll kneel
some moment beyond now. But know I'll feel
your slights until your pride and anger heal.

*

Adam:

How can I stand between an angel, great
as sea, as sky, as all the earth, and you,
who are my part, my fraction, bit. Untrue,
the ground on which I stand, then. You berate
the who I am, but angel waits, this weight
within the very am you hate. Through
and through our struggle here, we can't undo
the myth that rules us. It only can create.

But now we must relive forever. Now,
no matter how we disagree, our tale
will tell itself down through the flesh of each
we must become. And now you must allow
the angel's weight, and let the pain prevail
of one more taken rib, for what it teach.

    *

A father for them all, and I first cause.
So, new, a mother for a perfect race,
my blood ennobled by the Faceless Face.
This is the plan. It has (Beware!) no flaws!

(And though the garden will be closed, his brow
be glossed in sweat,
                his rage become the first
inheritance of murder,
                  though his thirst
in fields so scant of yields will keep his *how*
befuddled,
           his is not a face you'd kiss,
even know, among those children sung.

As for the other mother, can you heed her
there where she stands invisible among
the ligaments of earth, and lets your *here*
accept the gifts of wonder, joy, and fear?)

How Many Times the Echo?

And here they are again, as us, that you,
this me. Back at the house,
                              before we rode
in stiff, hurt silence to some goddamned do
we couldn't not attend, despite the load
of threat and barb unsaid,
                              she stood behind
your eyes, and he reared up in me: gods,
perhaps, or demons, surely, eating mind
and leaving ancient urges, those at odds
with what we'd hoped be cultured, civil, good.

We yelled the things we yelled,
                              we rode,
                                    we went
into the party where its drink and food,
its laughter, music, let the fit be spent.

Or sort of. Toes got tapped as we played tunes,
but every song seemed echoing from ruins.

*

Night, mid-dark, and you in that room, me
in this, the not quite unfamiliar bleed
of lights on window-facing walls you see
perhaps calls up her eidolon. I feed
my own anxieties, and wake each time
those headlights pass, the ones too shaky,
                                        late,
the hangers-on,
                    the far too drunk.
                                    The crime
they are about to be,
                    is it just fate?

And does this heart beat out *his* dance, a meat-
drum that all past has thonged tight on the frame
of what I must, because I sport discrete
proof of him here, balls in a sac,
                                    if tame
enough that you can wake
                    or sleep,
                                    that next
room over, snore safely, other sexed?

The New Kittens

A mere,
    a thistle down,
        a handful with sharp
bits half of which betoken desire,
as Afghan factions together make dispute
near perfect,
        purring, chomp on thumb web
soft enough to pull away, oh, kitten,
if I give my heart, how soon the death
of squirrel at wood pile!
            That,
                in this night,
your warmth so near my throat, how might you, small,
be path into the other?
            The war's so far,
and all the faces yet unkissed, who come,
rag-draped, home.
            Mewling for breakfast, and give
you a name? Then
            Ishtar, sacred whore,
and for your consort, Marduk, who will be,
castrated, all the senses of your *he*.

Wrong Number

That moment on the phone,
                    when nothing's there,
or fax beeps,
          and the voice you want
                         a whiff
of inter-,
          state or province,
                    you're not sure,
this continent's so complex
                    that a here,
                              if
truly *they* record,
               to better serve,

but who among us uses land-lines now,
and where am I,
               or you, plot-driven
character who can't even keep the nerve
to not hang up,
          and, I-numb,
                    you allow
the call to make no sense,
                    like name, given
to honour saint or elder,
                    and the kid
goes changing it to something you'd forbid,

a cruel joke, like Mr. and Mrs. Head
naming their son Richard,
                    and laughing till they're dead.

Good Xians All

The Vatican't, O Zinger of Rat,
your Vatican't, or won't, nor ought,
claims all that purple cored by rot!
if Reverend Larry took as toys
those deafly nubile, buggered boys,
and after who hushed up the noise?

Then what's the good of gold-wove sumption
if no one mitred's got the gumption
to put aside the sad presumption
of letting God sort out His own.

Decision's such a thorny crown.
But none have zung against the loss.

Go pull that Jew down from his cross!
Were he alive, you'd know who's boss!

*

Or was it that a Hitler youth
was so confused by right, by couth,
that you might *heil* a small mistruth?

As priest of the uncircumcised,
you knew your God's folks were despised,
yet you deemed sorrow ill-advised
for those who, heavenward as ash,
could urge a zeal do something rash.

Oh, bow your head; yes, bow it more.
So Babylon must have its whore;
the diddle-list stays in the drawer,
and all is calm as liturgy
well practised for the marks to see
your fearsome God is never free.

In the Style of Albert the Alligator

Oh, Baptists, my Baptists, the queers have your balls!
They've hung' em, with tassels, to *be*-deck their halls!
Be afraid! Be afraid! For the queers might just win!
Then God in His heaven won't let you come in!

The Jews, you are certain, killed Christ on a cross,
and what must you do now to show 'em who's boss?
By wrath, tribulation, and *su*-ggesting stones,
prepare 'em, that angels may dance on their bones!

But surely your Phelps is a saviour disguised
in tie, shirt and jacket, among the baptized,
the one most like Jesus, forgiving and fair,
for whom little perjuries cause no despair.

Topeka! Your Westboro sect too late hates
the *U*-nited Queerdom of these Homo States!

*

And here are the Texans buy books for our young:
McLeroy, the Gablers, and MinuteMan Ames,
the Offutt, the Barton, and those names among
the Christian Revisionists reffing the games
so *your* kid and *her* kid, that kid over there,
gets Godified goodness, that if were Islam,
a McLeroy in elsewhere would cry out despair,
would cry home his daughters, and who'd give a damn?

(For like it or not, with *our* towel-wrapped heads,
the rules on *our* side, and the might of *our* buck,
we'd know that Great Allah would succour our dreads,
and set, for our market, the worth of a frippery.

(If God made the world in Her wisdom for us,
of course She loved Darwin, in spite he was wuss!))

The Upshot of a Humanist Education

O, reader, my reader, go fiddle yourself!
The kittens have jumped behind books on the shelf!
If books are important, the kittens don't know,
and mostly I have 'em on shelves for the show!

The books are like God, Who's a Word in the night,
for when I have jitters, or some other plight,
and dread overwhelms me, and makes me accept
that I'm small and I'm helpless as losses I've wept.

They're whomped on the floor by a strong kitten kick,
in the night, in the fear, as a proof of the trick
that the world's really here, that I suffer in vain
to address in the mirror that fellow named Wayne!

And yet the soft bellies of kittens are such
as comfort distraction in stroking a touch.

F.... Centrism

You don't remember, but you're made of ash.
The huntsman found you, hoping for your heart.
He fed you to the wolf, who shat you out.
The fairy never promised any wish.

Deals of your stuff were forged in fusion cores.
And if you read this, rarely do you think
a woman much too intimate to thank
first gathered you, a self, from carbon's ores.

There's not much new about you, but for you,
so very small a part, for such great care.

Oh, yes, the moral: What of you proves rare
you'll waste, most like, but always call it true.

The fay's confirmed a fake, and stellar throes
by bits are you, again awaiting crows.

The Martyrdom of Claus

See, Santa was a sitting duck, his bum
one side some mike-space from the man whose jowls
were alcoholic five o'clock. 'You're red
from boot-tops to your head,' the grumble said,
as Santa sat. 'Come, sir, don't play dumb!
Our radar tracks your movements!' (*Shrieks and howls
of pinkos pincered offstage left.*)
                                (Oh, don't
cave in, dear Santa! though monsters hunt
witches who're as sham as you!)
                                    'We know you haunt
kids' dreams, with your naughty and nice, by dint
of your associations, those who'd daunt
with recognized brands, Coca-Cola, who'd hint
alternate lifestyles, Hollywood Jews,
                                    well, ain't
cuttin' it! Your jollies here aren't worth a cent!'

What Did the Incas Suffer,
Since No One Truthfully Wrote Them Up?

My brain makes claim on meaning. Nothing less
delights its silly jelly. Poke, poke,
a line, poke, triangle, all the dots

connected. When I tell you I confess,
I mean of course my brain, whose standing joke
is that it thinks it's me. It costs me lots,

some jobs, four kids, three mates, to say I bless
this world with my presence, but it's all smoke
and mirrors, brain pretending that the knots

in the message lace, brought so king can guess
the horror on his borders, pale folk
astride unknown beasts, are not just plots

by next of kin, or mountain god, the *Him*
by whose invention throats were cut, is whim.

Translated Heroship: The Price of Helping

There was a princely fellow wed a witch.

Why can't true love come off without a hitch?

The girl was from out East, and didn't know
the gratitudes a foreign bride should show.

When prince asked that his dad be cured of age,
her secrets did the job, but what a rage
when princely cousins tried the same, and dead
was nuncle. 'Get it through your Eastern head,'

he said, the prince, 'you can't go killing off
those very ones, that others may then scoff,
including shepherds with their whetted knives,
who have such interest in the princely wives

that they will cut a throat, instead of sac,
if they think bitch, not balls the prince might lack.'

*

The cat, so liquid in its skin (its wave
washed to her lap, where Egypt of its ear
she fondled) answered with bronze eyes. 'We draw
the gold within the stream by sinking hides.
You've saved those fleeces in your chests.' But witch
was not denied. She knew the herbs, the chants,
the measures of the maze of dance. He knew
the death she dried there in sight, for which names
he'd none. And there were tykes. How can a man
expect to live with such a horror? Gone
from her bed, a new bride (as was custom),
and before the fated could regain his head,
the bride, the father, kids, dead, the witch
fled. Pay heed, you with ring in pocket!

Regret

O lady, you're the dog-shit on my shoe!
No matter how I scrape, I'm never rid
of you. Of all the wrong you say I did,
surely only some of it smears true.

Surely there's exaggeration. Few
among those crimes seem likely. Though I hid
my tender soul from you, did I forbid
my other secrets? Make my heart tabu?

And what won't you admit? Oh, tit for tat,
the slanders of failed love! Yes, I did this,
but you'd done that! and done it for the hurt!

I talk to void, of course, a blank abyss
to which is stuck this bit of stink, the scat
of something past, the gossips' dirt.

A Little Nosegay to Carry through These Streets

When *is* the day the priests will thieve no rights
to rites, and freeborn souls have wrung the ring
of bell or blare of horn from those who've sung,
so wrong, the intercessions to those heights
where that Enthroned remarks the bribes and writs
by which priests prosper? When this lowsome rank,
of which I'm one, hope to talk unthunk,
sans garden, to You whose laughter at my wits
supposedly laughs love? This mendicant
who, rising from his grip-shone bowl, would nod
to, gladly, You, no need for any to mediate,
no prophet in a temple snug with God

(behaviour that in proles they'd medicate),

just chat with You, and no one think it odd?

The Barn Door on Trestles

It falls, the house, as broken-backed as horse
that would be to the knacker's. Apple trees
grown thigh-girth, sapped out by suckers. Freeze
and thaw, the barn's boulder footings forced
a-tumble from their settings, but the worst
is char of bearing timbers, lost ablaze
by roof-leaked rain in hay-mow, haze
of steamy smoke mixed with that morning's mist.

And likely ended what the farm had known.

For they were bride and husband in that barn,
before the house was done, the greening June
alive in garden, a field cleared as their own
by father, cousin, friends from down the way.

The sun grew sleek on wind-combed back of hay.

This memory's a fiction. If their lives
got shuffled into dust outlasting names
along the township road, well, no one claims
that history can be more than writing drives
the versions of our greeds. And what survives
the registry can't be enough to sort the blames
that after made rebuke about the flames,
until uncaring. The present's what arrives
from small forgettings, like her wedding ring
so grooved in fingerflesh and gone at death
down into muddled tales of earth, that you,
here reading, imagine it be just a thing,
a dull gleam around a bone. But your breath
makes this present a gift more than you knew.

Then peel some apples with the cooks. The skins
will be fermented by the men to booze,
something women peelers might then use
to cry the guilts, to quaver out as sins.

Among the peelings, seeds so brown as guess
a root-stock compromised for local choice,
given that the very air's salt-moist,
and no pig squeals, the sole bit lost.

The hawk's-bill knife pares out the rot
sweet brown as though the apple meat
all-readies itself for celebration, a feat
of flesh to wine, miraculous as old breasts
past suckling these thirsty, gulping-last-year's men
admire, though it's with peelings they conspire.

Oh, not just rinds. The scabbed, and windfalls, too,
and more than half a share of sound, to press
a goddess sweetness from, and foam a mess
that, strained and kegged a few weeks on, 'll renew
a faith in mutability. Brought through
in a cool cellar, a last cask to bless
this latest freshness of the Lady's *Yes!*
to jubilation, that the harvest's true.

The larded chops put down in crocks, the sides
and hams to smokehouse, mince and work the stuff
of sausage, no, nothing of this abides.
They're gone, who were that laughter, were that rough.

Besides, this present so fills what I write,
you hear the highway grumbling through the night.

3 a.m.

Waking, the night-dark still window hungry,
still whispering trash light. No, the dream's
left behind, a wife and children angry,
hurt you disappeared from a home where seams
between this and other unravel, and they'd
needed you to stay. The bed smells like bed,
the house beyond it all the more emptied.
You've lost already the last words they said.

Turn on the lamp. Get up. What was the scent,
her nape? Put on the kettle. No use now.
A girl and boy that looked like you, like her.
No matter where hereafter you lie down,
you'll never find them, nor the broken road you went
to lead you back. Only this house is sure.

Waiting for the Queen Car

Nowhere on maps of loss is marked that spot
the cleft mountain opens to Shangri-La.
Nowhere's x'ed that place, helplessly far,
the fountain pools your face. What you've got
is your confusion, the late nights you've bought
into, the short-cuts on the job, the raw
streetlight anointing a stranger's eyes, the air
too used, the dread that can't deny you're caught.

Poor pink-eyed rat! You're cancers in waiting, lusts
invented by the signage, warrened in stacks!
The maze turns right or left, is never *here*,
is never any shame but tedium or fear
that draw the maps of loss to show your tracks
defeated by the scourings, grits, the dusts.

The Martyrdom of Claus: The Best Defence Is …

I keep a long knife by my bed to scare
off night-brought felons. The not bright
I'll hand back their heads. I practise, days,
on melons. *Thunk*, goes razor steel thru rind.

One swipe's all I need to stop the goons
that creep as night-fears up my stairs to catch
me napping. But my worries, as I'm drifting, bring
me back to shadows. Money. Love. Lack of.

So time a-bed's a Christmas waiting, Nick
in German, and his smutty fiend, Krampus,
friend! Friend! I have misspelt! A creak!

The stairs! Where's my knife? I've left it in
the kitchen by the murdered melon! Quick!
Quick! Here come tall boots. Heels click!

A Workable Venus

We can't agree on how
to make the bed. You tuck.
I like to leave some toe-room
free. You'll pull the covers up.
I like to see the sill's geraniums,
how light gets fed across
the lifelines of each leaf.
Instead of winter's slant,
you want the mystery
of muzzy blowhole
nuzzled shapelessly
about your nose
so I'll guess
your hid head.

Then why's it me
who dreams the underside
of sea-ice, sun-shaft plankton
swirling motes, the whole embrace
of pressure? so I rise
to breathe what only breath
can here confide, the waking
whispers ready in our throats.
Your eyes open, open
without surprise.

In these few days,
the paint's become the wall.
A matter of some names,
and how we see. Or name
the seeing, that we can agree
the wall looks so much better.
Where the fall of sunlight seems
so clean is still the wall,
but paint has dried beyond
its name, is free of any sense
but colour. It was we who filled
and brushed and rolled, now
must recall where nick was,
scuff was, smudge, below the skin
of name that covers them. If soon
enough fresh paint records
our clumsy lives as stuff
of knock and rub, a surface
marred to *in,* how can we think
its namelessness to blame?
Does all that needs a naming
know its name?

I know the weight
of a sleeping child's arm,
will, after, guess it still,
the mass of night
humped up the breath-stitched stairs,
weight right for such a child, this
sleeping child. No harm will come,
what harm might come, oh,
please, no harm, they're only
stairs up into dark, so light
a load, in fact, despite the stitch,
the tight across the small of back,
no need alarm the child who'd wake and struggle,

eased a-bed as heaviness
I'd have climbed higher for,
and, sliding from shoulder,
arm's lax embrace become
fingers curled on palm instead,
just that, a holding on to nothing. More
we can't hang onto, if this leaves no trace.

The window on the landing
looks out west. The light
late afternoon falls in so clear,
the orchid's spot-lit bloomlessly
sincere on Uncle Allen's corner stand.
Impressed, I stop mid-flight
to let the light suggest
that later I'll have nothing
I need fear when this light
has gone and dark's here,
when coming up these stairs
portends a rest

needful, says dark,
though there's so much
to do, urgent, says dark,
though I'd sooner not lie down
just yet, not have orchid leaves
curl black against the wall's dimness.

'Oh, turn,' say you, 'the landing light on,
rather than!' and frown, as though
the dark were simply light's lack.

If doing dishes warms my hands,
then why as I'm standing here
with the warm drape of water
over knuckles do I think
of your nape, the fragile hairs
thereof? My hands would pry,
if you were standing here,
your braid awry that bit to tease
your huff, let strays escape
enough that I could blow
a tickle's scrape so lightly
you'd give up to teasing, sigh.
Then I'd give up and kiss your nape.
You'd smile. There are some truths
so easy to predict, the speculation
is as good as act. If you'd come
in this kitchen, catch me while
I smile my daydreamed teasing,
would you have picked the moment
just to see how I'd react?

You went out and left the radio on
upstairs. I thought I heard these voices.
If I heard voices, where, the open window?
Blurred chatter, insistent, eager,
bringing affairs of consequence here,
now, as are our cares to us argued,
teased, if not so spurred to fill air-time.
And that's how I was lured
upstairs alone, and found the voices
theirs,
         these strangers talking
strange concerns, not ours.
A thousand times I've talked with you
right here. This room we thought,
when kids moved out, was spare,
now where we both make and do,
the hours passing twilight,
lamplight contracting near,
our voices silent, focus
sagged to stare.

You're breathing there. But words,
if mortal, too, and other, as
your mouth speaks these alive,
these very I had hoped you'd let
arrive on tongue-tip, so, with bits
of me as you, you'd know this speaking
is an act of love.
                  Those moments past
in which a dark might thrive,
a calming dark, its voice repeating
true its comfort in the shifts
that snag recall as it gropes back
along forgotten's wall, you know
those moments, and the voice thereof.

It isn't that the stories in the dark,
repeated past their meanings
to that spark the voice itself was,
would speak for what is all.
The world can't be so safe.
But words will do.

The Prolonged Sadness of Belief

Cliché the First

There was a little boy who thought true love
was hopeful real, not Santa fake, nor tooth
fairy tale, nope, whole cloth he'd sleuth
out, when he learned how.
                              But boy must live,
and take what scraps allowed; from them will suture
the monstrous double the man'll keep alive
in dungeons of his dreams, allowed no leave
except to squish through sewers of a future.

That Caliban would crush the hand-held Rhonda
from grade three, distill from throb-slim Linda
one spoiled sneer, and cleave, Ah! peevish Vera,

the hope into its sunders.
                              So when a wife
I do-ed beside him, he felt what scruffy stuff,
this hand-me-down, must suit him for a life.

Cliché the Second

An old man rocked on his own porch,
his wives and children gone, the dog dead.
What *was* that tune kept humming through his head?
What *was* the distance, bled out from this perch
where all his world was centred, that it hid
the harms the creature from dream's cellars did.

The many moments man can blame will parch
his skin, and thicken eyes, and kill the pooch.

But what was sentimental when he'd had
the scents of different women in his bed,
the nothing sense that no man had to heed,
true as her child voice, true as it boded
recognition, one he'd never made
of red-haired Rhonda in his gone third grade?

Another Evening at the Movies

Never trust a yellow-brick girl,
a mid-rung, me-first, brick-church girl,
a youngest of church-weddings girl, the one
who never would get caught, and baked a whole
swot of special brownies (mom ate two
and was so very sleepy, there's no place
the mind don't roam), a bit of theft, a moue
of fun, a shower quick between the day's
beaux, and so to bed.

                        'It's yours!' she said.

There's that professor Dietrich tricks to clown
in film so old, who cares? That when the town
red-painted woke with sniggers to the head
pain-repentant, pointed, pointed, a belly
swelling – poor old prig après-beer smelly.

Tantrum

I want the one whom I was promised, long
before this breath began, long before
death even noticed I'd become a man.

I want the one whose pores were whitened with
the exudate of child. I want to be
held by the moment thinking hasn't failed.

I want the mild, unreasoned giving makes
the worth of earth seem whole; I want the sake
of love convinces me I'm not a fool;

the she who'd be my own completion, strong
as guessing, tough as lies, the she who wakes
my whole, caressing all this self as dies.

I want the one be at the ending, wise
with God's own mostfelt passion, close my eyes.

Jeremiad

When I could've said, 'No,' and reason win.
Beautiful, clear and painful reason. Begin
a world with reason, and there *is* no sin.
There's only reason shining its childish grin.
There's no you, my counter, seen first
with someone else more pretty, who was cursed
with wanting to be cared for, and a thirst
for middle-class values, then the worst
start out of that. But reason'd have no want.
No horrors waking dark. So nonchalant
was reason that it didn't know the taunt
as taunt, and so the world began anew
askew, and all the same old hurts'd do,
in reasonable time, for me, a you.

Philippic

Ah, you're the traitor snuck into my bed
pretending this old body caught your spark
that ended with my ashes hauled. Instead,
you closed your eyes, though we were in the dark,
and never called a name I didn't know.
Why *is* it women think they're better whores
than men can ever pay them for, and grow
the bolder in the shucking of their drawers
the more they ask. I've paid out with my heart,
of course, though it was bankrupt from the first,
and, given it's a chattel, never part
of Ponzi scheme that's made this trading worst.

Ah, you, with the compassion of a stone,
with banker's smile, let me die alone!

The Enchantment

Because the sorceress lacked for blowfish dust,
she improvised with mac and cheese and many,
many eggs she claimed the perfect food.

The sorceress hid in frowsy floral prints,
second-hand, so as not to draw notice.

Murky of mind, I changed babies by nights.
I always came back from where I'd gone out.
I don't remember if there was money, but,
before, the sorceress'd bought good drugs.

When I wouldn't take one, she gave another.
Of course I'm a good person. Who is not,
to the small self inside, a good person?

My past selves all turned swine, thick
with trickery, heartfelt mute to those they'd loved.

*

Her vengeance was to prove she didn't care.
I was peeling a potato. I held it to my temple
and whispered 'Bang!' The sorceress said, 'Go mad,
and I'll have to get rid of you!' I put the loaded
potato down. The sorceress said, 'You can't
drink anymore.' My thirst itched from throat
to balls. Foggy of intent, I went out to meet
a perfect husband. I was well trained. I put
out my hand to shake his. 'Perfect!' he said.
It hadn't seemed so complicated a question.
Perfect lover? Perfect gentleman? I was
a perfect zombie, my heart a crushed beer
can. My will was a wineglass set down
on the walk back from nowhere and forgotten.

The goddess rode me, jealousy and lust.
I wanted so a she concrete in truth
that all my friends would wonder at my couth
in having made the perfect match. But dust
rose up and choked me blind. I knew disgust
was at some core awaiting, as the lost
will ever wait, until the shore exhaust
the unreturning ship's horizon. Most,

you'd guess, would take to life-boats, rather than end
with cops on the lawn. Nice cops. Good cops.
Oh, guard my head to put it in the back!
Oh, guard my soul, in hopes that it might mend!
Oh, talk the code and wail through all the stops!
As though I'd hold my breath, die of that lack!

*

Any life depends on space, a castle
condo cottage cave a fastness where
the I is so, if even just that small
its walls rub shoulders with the earth. And what
a hassle, coming back from where the scraps
of grief have sucked themselves as dry as heaves,
and mind was presence far beyond what pills
could find no hole for.
                          The sorceress had another
stiff fed eggs, fed orange cheese, fed stodge,
before the month was up. Already jealousy
clouded his thick glasses. I spent a long
time coming back from the dead. The face
in the mirror lip-synched every false confession.

If after, to be dead again. What peace!

A Wakeful Night at Little Bob's Lake

Hwas Annie's gone stare into sun flicker
off the water at late supper, the day's lived-
long and mostly-loud piling up
the west as darkness.
              There was I as father
parsing out my care as I could give
between three hungry, tired pups,

and there was, as a mean while, back at the ranch,
a woman sulking on her motherhood
with latest babe she'd wanted to avoid.

The stars started sticking down each hunch
of ancient light, probing as they could
to find our wonder staring up at void

and them to bed,
                  kids' breathings, along
with crickets, frogs,
                      a lonesome, whiskied song.

The Necessity of Dedication

For Don McKay. For Victor Coleman. Steve
McCaffery. For George Bowering. For Michael Oh!
For Brian Bartlett. Al. For who believe
the CC grants by goodness. For no
associate member. For mentorees from Banff.
For *Best of* anthologists. For three-named
poetesses. For the lessons funded chairs have.
For smart-mouthed attitude. For claiming 'famed'
or 'noted' or 'prize-winning', especially in site
entries. For declarative sentences with pretension to verse.
For MFA programs. All whose right
to write I will not judge. I'd make things worse.

I stick a bandaid on a kid's scraped knee,
for it's a doctor that makes me!

Required Coursework

The univers(e)it(ill or all)y each fall
offers for pro(and con)fessional poets
(those short-listed, anthologized, those juried)
a blurb-writing course, to be taught by a team
with close ties to fully funded publishers.

The applicant has excessive mentoring of his
(or her)stories, and current membership in
at least three recognized support or(der!
Ordure!)ganizations (see list appended).

The course will explore enlightened word choices
(brilliant! luminescent! incandescent!),
and hyperbole of vatic and incantatory natures.
Coteries are invited at group rates. A non-
refundable honesty is payable in advance.

The Rules of Engagement

BushMaster 2-6

The scope reduces everything. No smells
down there, no after-poignant aftershave.
Just slightly overweight Iraqis, armed
with satchels, thoroughly afraid. And Kyle,
the trigger man, so high on *whup whup*
whup I just want to kill me some towel
heads (pretend your uncle down there, your dad,
what does it take, you dumb, scope-blinded
fuck, outside the bullshit football talk,
the vidgame talk, your brother, your other breath
in the dark, who shared a mirror), Kyle, you're
the only named. Wuh, Wuh, Wuh,
your chief exec. You go to hell for everyone,
since Wuh, Wuh, Wuh's his father's son.

Gun Camera

I know, I know, that whole approach is rant,
agitprop unfit for decent verse.
And picking out just one to be the cunt
who does the killing, when the whole of force
flies up, an unstopped buck, to Warlord George,
beyond, to Saud, to Prophet's profit, fierce
as spent uranium, O Dollar, purge
in so ascending every wrongful farce,
and keep the oil flowing in the pipe!
And, Greenback, mightier than Allah, curse
dissenters' eyes that they see horrors worse
than they can tell! America is ripe!
There is no moral! Sunday school was cant!
O Dollar, spare no quarter! Hear my rant!

Alright. Hahaha

You don't like Nazis, do you? Killed the Jews,
no matter Jews control the Street, and keep
such Hollywood alive as takes your cash,
keeps you poor so that you join, and seep
your blood out in foreign dust, use
your very stuff towards their wealth. Trash,
they call you, laughing to the bank. So cheap,
your labour, meat-cheap, or did you confuse
commodity with honour, stumps for flash?
(Look at me not wiggle toes!)
                                    She calls
these my diatribes, the woman who does
my dirty laundry. Rinsing out my smalls,
she makes a comment on the House of Saud,
and oil monopoly, and shooting wad.

Parents! Buy Your Kids Video Games!

Hotel 2-6. Come on, let us shoot!
Please say we can shoot. We want to shoot!
Big daddy, we need to shoot now!
We need to shoot these towel-heads, and how!
I go to the market where the women shop.
I take my machete and begin to chop.
I go to the playground where the children play.
I take out my machine gun and begin to spray.
Oh, yeah, look at those dead bastards!
Nice. Goddamn it, Kyle. It's their
fault for bringing their kids to a battle. One
guy crawling around down there.
Drove over a body! Really! Hahaha
I hit 'em. Crazy Horse 1-8.

Ethan McCord

has kids of his own, and drops them at school in Amer-
ica. Ethan McCord has a letter on line
written in best-shot, spell-checked Amer-
ican. McCord, did he vote? Who for? W?
And who commanded Ethan McCord? What
is a war crime, daddy? We don't learn a thing
in school about. Will men in choppers come
to kill us? 'Amer' means bitter. Bitter, bitter,
the flashbacks of Ethan McCord. Hitler was loved
by smiling crowds, don't you remember? Amer-
ica is bitter, bitter, losing wars,
as bitter as Starbuck's grounds of fine Arab
-ica, free market gung-ho. And who
might Ethan McCord be? Good shootin'. Thank you.

Sleeping Late into the Morning

Dream before so late a waking
seems the more intense for staring
down the beast of such a pairing,
four-armed, four-legged. Forsook.

Nothing dreamt can harm me, nothing
lies within the dream but taking
sad symbologies of aching
lust-bound. Doubt-sound. Mistook.

She I loved and he for hating
went about their perjured mating
as they must have on that evening
late home. Blame howled. Trust shook.

John Donne! how disbelieving
can't repair a grieved deceiving!

The Martyrdom of Claus: Flue Blockage

If Santa's in the chimney, stuck, because
I don't believe, if Santa's summoned up
the pluck, but now I've got a peeve, the flaws
in such an argument, besides the cup
of joy and cakes and cost thereof, the fuss
of desiccated corpse removal, show
for certain the gullibility of us
who want god up the flue. The answer NO
is so alone, and death that much more weird,
a life's absurd. I'd just as well ascend
the high tower, dole out what's a-feared
with stolen rifle, oh, bring their decent end.
For, after all, we'd shoot a broken horse.
Though slugs won't heal a broken soul, of course.

Caliban Grown Old

A private creature children sly for who
is egg my master marvelled scrambled is
Plato untold if love emerges true
but too became a limp to frighten crows

as dimpled trance she stretched withon the moss
to show her belly's most suggestive span
unblemished hand's breadth of pursing skin
that guise in pool's reflection prove my loss

my loss my loss and if I moaned her beast
there blanched in tilth I would bewooded man
without but words from her to child the feast
my world *is* of master's evil none

my own got borne who breathe as well divine
and hold my caring child her still within.

Miranda, after Ferdinand's Desertion

Before my father, anger with your claim
you would have peopled that small world through me ...
well, father's judgment saw I must fix blame
that moment, for the moments we'd been free
beyond his plans ... that sorcerer, who kept
a sprite of wind to keep his will, condemned
the balance of the monster.
                              So I wept
to witness whippings. And after, skirting hemmed
by mud, my way cave-ward to your moans,
I lost the danger in a love that moved
beyond the need to comfort. She who owns
her fate is richer far than she who's proved
another's star-knot is her only chance
for height. In that past, dance, monster, dance.

Caliban Bemoans

That I am ugly, mad and fat, and neck-
bent to this elder patience, life's the beck
which call I serve to death, its utmost check
without a hope for mutiny to wreck
me, chancy new the like of never seen
before and so a comely wonder, mien
to rule my island own and you for queen
and never will or love some fate to wean,
not ugly as these lines half twist to true
and half that lie all dreaming makes desire
that I not touch as beast the inward you
and you not take my rough as you require
a handsome tenderness until the yew
might suckle from our stuff the stuff of fire.

Miranda Pretends to Be Every Woman
Who's Ever Loved the Bad Boy

Well, no, the title isn't true at all.
You know it's me, the author, lurking here
behind the lines, far from danger, small
as any humans are, who suffer fear
they'll be found out they're not among the brave
up at the front. And Caliban a sleaze.
I loved a girl (Linda! The spotlights rave
through waving arms stopped in the strobe's frieze
and white her stark, so slim, so pouty, proud
she's been picked out, but shy to be the there
to every here all staring). Nope. She avowed
a tattooed thug, so smug with buff, and hair
that Will'd have written in, for he knew sluts
and what they liked, all whiffs, all hands, all butts.

That Small Lie about the Soul

That once the mind gets used to it, the meat
seems unimportant (fingers needn't grasp
what never could be held beyond the beat
of heart, the push and pull of breath to clasp

too strongly (life's a greed that makes no sense
for any restless ghost (for once the mind
unthinks its here, and gives to the immense
the inmost that had found itself confined

(a here behind the eyes, and serving one
when all so calls from distance to include
the back of being, where the mask, begun
in so much all, now fails to be renewed))))

and ghosts haunt our imaginations where
we know there's closed and sole and unbreathed air.

The Ghost in the DNA

Did no one warn you about the pretty pictures?
The ones well-chosen words are so good with,
the incantatory rhythms, tonal mixtures
meant to touch you? And though she's never stood with
you at a sunset when the light's leaning strictures
blurred both your faces so handsome, the stark
west cloud-crowded gold, its textures
resembling bared skin before its dark
closes the world and dissolves your perfect lover,

she you'd hoped for more than great-grandmother
with whom you also haven't stood, but unmooted
since straightforwardly you're here, and bother

to want love in this world in which you're rooted,
a perfect love, yours, and undisputed?

The Tattoos in the Parking Lot

It's not the gates are tested by the horde.
What passed in, here, among, some time ago,
illiterates producing books for bored
and boring commentators, culture show
for well-fed reviewers,
                            fuck, rappers
as the usual TTC crap, spilling
out of earbuds, dog turds, gum wrappers
at the stops,
                and these stops, *ding*, distilling
the moment you stand down to night, the tic
of ozone overhead, and, *rrrrrr*, its delete
down tracks to leave you in aloneness, thick
as prod to move you, *tzach!*, along the street.

They're here. They breathe around you, speak that tongue
the bogeyman bespoke, when you were young.

It's Only Po Tree,

Can, eh? jun, at that,
means a modernishy multimush, head
office in Toronto. About this bush
high culture beateth not, key
of *I* flat. Or *'we'* intimate, to fool
the boobs into believing *'we'* like 'em, just
a bit. But, jeez, look, *'we'*"re potes! *'We'*
can get government grants! if 'our' *'friends'* ref
'our' documents! And 'they' do, 'they' want, 'themselves'!
Oh, po-eh?-tree for po-Ms' sake, if deaf
to music and the ethical a-loooo-
shon, lookit up, 'you' safe and daft 'you'
who want, who want, who want, there's nothing left
but plots of sheep on hillside, wordsheared deft.

Ammonite, Geode, Meteorite, Man

A ram's-horn curl, pyrite-coated, broken
from dark matrix, a marine erosion, tiny
white barnacles on the back. Jurassic.

An earth egg, half-sawn, the curls of agates
miming sea-waves breaking over rock,
small sparkles of facets rough enwombed.

Thumb-end-sized brown-blackened glassy
bit, pitted and smoothed by frictioned air,
a piece of very other, beyond my guessing.

With a Dordogne hand adze, my true antiques.
The youngest is a hundred thousand years,
the oldest a hundred and seventy-five million.

Sixty-three times I've been around
Great Angel Sun. Do the math.

A Fable

The wise accumulate stupidities.
Not knowing better what to do, they force
mistakes through to those sad houses of cards
their hearts are. Oh, the songs of the wise
as they make their work are silly as commands.
They note the sizes of their friends' hands,
compare their breathing, hum, badly, and the hum
is swarm in their hearts of cards. They dealt none
but that the edges stung, blunders they came by.
Oh, the wise dance when they see their friends nimble!
Their own stumbles shake down their hives of hearts.
The wise, their failures gather at the fumble
of sweetness sprung on them by their surprise:
that trust of fellow where the sting most smarts.

Metaphysical Desire

For J. Z.

What magic makes is gullible belief.
How sad we must confess the simple fate
that Santa Claus has gone. If god is great,
if needful mercy salves some cool relief
on living's burning itch, however brief,
if gone, then where? with all that Santa weight
in our imaginations, perfect bait
for faith, to make one's death a lifelong grief....

So lit.'s all charming wit and well-turned phrase?
You never once believed in Santa Claus?
Then close this book. You've not deserved the charge
of having found, within the glamoured maze
beneath the tree, your tag-writ name made pause
the celebration, and your *self* come large.

The Exile at His Window

One here and now, Pythagoras struck strings
to chords that sang the weaving into things
of vital restlessness all time-drawn brings;

and bloodied, naked Christ stretched out his arms
a here and now to who beheld the harms
done on his flesh, to solace their alarms;

if Joan, unlettered, made her Dauphin fear
a woman might persuade the Holy's ear
to hear in screams of flame her now, her here,

or daughter choose forget a father's gift
(if generation knots its line with *if*,
invests a recklessness of faith as rift),

then he is done with views, and how Fish Point's
a here so poorly *now*ed as disappoints.

The Horizon Starts from My Couch

Amelia Earhart flew down through my dream.
The sea-filled sea cast back a zenith glare.
Her noplace was too engine-dinned to scream;
her only island was the dazzle where
the sun crushed waves an oblong, hammered bronze.
The wingtips pointed to the circled edge
that drew the limit for those never dawns
jittering down to empty on the gauge.

A nap one afternoon. A purring cat
curled uncial on my chest. Flying's such
a Freudian gesture of the unthought-out.
And I'm a guy who hasn't travelled much.

But I've been very lost, no doubt of that.
Nor do I know the spot I'll have to ditch.

The Exile Meets Dante

The dream is so conventional. My eyes
are sewn shut, and my clothing, even my skin,
the shades of soil. I've left my box of why's
checked at some vast lost and found wherein
all boxes pile to narrow-alleyed walls
that hold back regret, or hope, or care.
I stand, to be not ground. I hear the calls
of fellows, but when I reach, they swirl to air,
their dust scouring my thirst. Thus I'm alone
amongst a many, waiting by the edge
of great things and far distances, a stone
taste on my tongue, when who should walk the ledge
but the real poet, the one I envy, he
whom luck chose a thousand years to be.

*

And walking with his mentor, heathen who
so served his state, the medieval mind
accepted that, as thought-wraith, he renew
a hope in hell for anyone maligned,
for those who spoke against the mucky-mucks,
for all those pinched between a wage and boss,
the ones who'd suffered I-don't-give-a-fuck's
from higher primates, those whose worthless loss
eked out the increments of frayed despair.
My fellows in the ring. The ones who moan.
The little folk a Laureate might compare,
while waiting for a train, to height his own,
as he once did, in Kingston, while I stood,
his driver, host, the scribe who'd scribed his good.

The Laureate, bespectacled like I'm,
a-smile that his tax dollars got returned
as wages for his governmental time,
an office in for free, the trips unearned,
but jet fuel burned for good, therefore wrote
officially, predictably, of stinky chain
saws. And who'll be we, this ring, to gloat
to see him dragged past on his way to pain?

The Poet paused to note me. 'Sad you chose
a birth among barbarians. But don't
embrace your envy of him. Unlike for those
deserving, nothing's there you'd want. Won't
you give up suffering and come with us?
There's so much for us sinners to discuss.'

*

If, since my high school Latin, I've been shy
with those more fluent, getting, say, the joke
Catullus, in so easy scansion, 'd try
to pack into a nose-length, for a poke
at Fabullus, when I had mumbled it
again, again, before I had it right,
well, there he stood before me, with the Pit
encompassed in his mind, and every plight
remembered in its place. He spoke. My tongue.
'Those vengeances you'd have all miss the point.
Whatever you might hope for here among
the dead, as due, would surely disappoint.
Unseal your eyes and strip your dunning off.
You free yourself when you can say, "Enough!"'

So I, a true Canadian, up-rose,
and followed, yes, that Great, that Good. For true
Canadians follow; such their fate. Just pose
the question to the Laureate. How you do
that, given he's seemed dead inside his smile
for several changes of the House, is moot.
While Laureate's lacked no smallish trick for style,
(he even named his mag *DRUT* (so cute
in mirrors (of which he built his smoky house)),
he'll only answer academics or Black
Mountain Men or maybe Beats, and grouse
about reviews suggesting he's a hack....

'If nothing can be learned, there's ignorance,'
said Virgil. 'When nothing will be, that's pretence!'

*

And chastened, I fell in behind. 'It's he!'
the Poet teased, 'from Emmaus' road.' The dead
should be more decorous, I thought. 'He'll see
it's fragments of one consciousness, instead
of any unifying theme. Yes, God
is great, but She proves late, and means to be!'
O, Christ, whined I, the infidel, I'll plod
another story out before I'm free.

They paused. They turned and looked. 'Including you,'
the Poet said, 'in our descent as more
than reader will not make its telling true.
Come here. Were you so better off before?'

I stepped up to his left, convinced my will
was naked as the path that fell downhill.

There on that crag, the Poet asked me why
he'd found me in that ground reserved for lust.
'The skinny girl you loved, did you not try
convincing her you were just whiles from dust?'

I cringed. I told him of my dog, her death,
of how she'd roused from suffering to howl
her presence to the antecedents breath
had made her: RaaaahAaaaaahrrAaaaaaahhrAaahhll!....

The Poet bowed his head. I couldn't tell
if sobs or chuckles bobbed his frame, but grief
is what I felt, and more for dog in Hell
than any skinny girl could bring relief.

The Poet asked whom else I'd loved, for zeal,
he said, might give the victim chance to heal.

                *

The chthon of gravity pulls down the dead
who act, since acting mocks the living. Three
dream-entangled agonists, one in dread,
slid and clutched at nothings down that scree.

At bottom we were met by one so gross,
I failed to recognize my former boss
until her toad-like form was standing close,
magnificent with every human loss.

'I know you!' was her greeting. So I shied
behind the Poet, who, with charming grace
explained I'd been unconscious since I died,
and didn't know the signs within her face.

She pouted. She up-pulled suspenders, snapped
her judgment. I'd pass, so long as I proved apt.

We trekked across a plain of stinking filth,
I skipping over parts of whore and pig
that any Willie Pickton'd plough to tilth,
The gluttons iced below my grisly jig
implored with frozen eyes. The other two
just walked, without much care for those beneath.
A fecal drizzle fell, a dungy dew
congealed our footprints on that anguished heath.

The hours became the days. The days lost track
of which they followed; frightened, flocked to weeks.
The elder two were silent. I looked back
at times, because I'd drawn ahead. The reeks
were just as choking, fresher, though, until
I came upon a glutton her own hill.

*

Immense she sat. Although her lower parts
were locked in shit-flecked ice, above, her flesh
swelled out each sag. She spoke, in obscene farts,
I thought a language, but it didn't mesh
with any that I knew. A filthy rag,
draped from a lanyard knotted round her neck,
hid one grotesque nipple. 'It was her flag,'
the Poet said, approaching, 'but the wreck
she proved as country, gorging on the world,
has brought her here.' I looked again. 'It's Miss
America, my stares come snipes unfurled!'
Said Poet, 'A country's soul has come to this!'

(No puns! I pled elsewhere to dream magic,
No easy morals, comedy turned tragic!)

'But what's a country doing here, and how'd
she get so BIG!?' I asked. 'Oh, out of many,
one,' said Poet, 'incorporate and loud.'
'A Simpsons' diet,' Virgil judged, 'an any
rather than a none at all.' 'You watch
The Simpsons?' I asked, wary. 'Of course,' said Seer.
'If anyone would understand the botch
those States became, he'd know Duff beer.'
'But this is Hell!' I cried. 'There's no TV!'
'Electromagnetic radiation,' sneered
Seer, ''s impossible to dodge.' That's when he
pressed that spot between my eyes. Weird!
Six seasons of *The Simpsons* in one touch!
I'd never known I'd liked Lisa so much....

*

Plump America, Fat New Found
policy to extirpate the Taliban,
strategized by your own spooks! Did George's pound
of almost unadulterated, ground
and maintenance-dosed, hormonal beef pan
out? The National Debt justify its grand
hot-doggedness? Its half-cooked plan,
akin to TV football, save the land?
At least for Republicans? Was Wall Street
brought forth from its hole-duggedness?
The bonuses paid out, the greed replete?
Had Generals and CEOs in smuggedness
junketed Congressmen who'd vote to cede
Cuban cigars for those with greatest need?

A dream's descent to horror's nothing new.
We human critters have been monster-fraught
for generations more than Ussher knew
among his sums. That guardsman at Kent State,
the one who aimed at Sandra Sheuer's neck,
as comely as a white-tailed doe's
                              (oh, you
must have your monsters in the dark. You ought,
if dreams hold out for justice. While she walked
to class, a speech therapy student bled out
before she had a chance to teach you what
you needed for a love that wasn't fuck
or kill) has anonymity as luck.

This side of a border without sense,
I suffer that your hunger's so immense.

*

It's just dream, a dirty, unreal place,
convincing in that sleep has nothing else
but nothing, so like death, where you've no face
in any mirror. Besides, you're mirrorless.
And it's not you who're dead. You're reading this.
In what sense you're awake helps sort the loss
that I must be, since now you can dismiss
the poet as the poet's double-cross.

So, here. Awake. The Laureate's moved on.
The decent cribs of Dante in your tongue
are flawed in ways you'd never think as wrong.

And Virgil's read no more. The classics lose
in every funding scrum, and Latin froze
three generations back, a blackened rose.

If Allen Ginsberg was a symptom, not
a poet (slippery slope, that WCW
said as much, didn't he? hater of iambs),
America so wanted a verse to call its own,
it let Walt Whitman take it in, as not
to be surprised when hanging chads for W.
so lowered standards, any use of iambs
became not much a notion that it own.

Oh, can a Da of kids as diff'rent as
a frenchifying element, and queen-
on-quarter stampers, those seditious states
not over yet the owning fellows as
their chattels (listen how this I berates)
accept a Pound of Tom for what it's been....

*

'Ha!' you say. 'You're that kind! A Pound's worth
of scraps always starting the Great Quilt,
the whole of a world stitched up that if I squint,
the seams blur. Cosmopolite of earth!
Word serf! How didn't Tommy Stearns'
misogyny make clear you need to Howl
more?'
        I'm shy and proud, know bullies, scowl
cowled, for a happy boy attracts their mirth.
If I won't be fat among the well-fed,
I'll sport their sloppy garb to hide my unlike.

You who don't care I've the good sense
to understand my trail has never led
this way before, pard, for your sake,
shut me up, your own path's that intense.

Sitting Around with the Greats

Ez

& Ez sang no goddam if readers owned
no Greek, nor Mandarin, no Roman, nor
re-bus(in-esse AEgyptae), archaic ranted,
grum bled hi story all borrowed vanity, 'a pom
puss cunt,' pretender to celebratty
and preacher to skool docters, the false confurtive,
the whoheknew his secret of excess,
and went down under the law's keel.
Mad, mad and pathos-caged eyeshut,
poor post-war bear who'd usured all
fine utterances so readers'd owe *him*,
but the music so poor (try sing it. No! *Sing*
it!) even allowed a radio Hecture of hump-
backed inglese to the troops, the Wops.

Pit Stop

A tattoo in cute kanji in the back
unseeable to whom therefore it marks
except in mirrors which are therefore life.

Old Dead Ez, you were false passage
to such, the tigers, powers in the ink,
and struck into the skin, if not the page.

Since no one'd trade a weary fuck about
your erudition except those on their way
to what ticket allows teachingflextime,

here, next pisser at Timmy's, Sackville,
'How are you today' eying my pecker,
two silver hoops in left ear,

writ small between his skittish eyes.
'Twas for such, Ez, your route still lies.

Spring in Southern Ontario Is Very Much
Like Interest in Canadian Literature

Grete Rude Stone upon her breathded said,
'then what's the question?' A comfort to me. Said
to've said, but get it right? Hard to be
someone else's daughter. Isn't she
expected to? Me? I met a lady poet
couldn't forgive me Spooner's syndrome. But.
But but but drunk she's ded too. All said
out. 'N' me, so 'ld 'm aforesaid.

Today's air's heavy with wet. The snow's
thaw's unbalding grass and splats a fat
firtree drop on noggin: I'm alive.
She didn't have to ask for Alice. Those
were answers were her life were pat, and what
I want to know is, why's more asked than I've?

Lisbon, 30 November, 1935

The many-headed Pessoa's trunk of verse
was loaded for love's voyage, but had no true
heading. Among so many stickers, perverse
there'd be none for destination, unscuffed clue
about a port. That bogus caucus in the poet's
noggin was every each a twist of him,
but, should he leave behind convincing quotes,
the steerage mind of world might take on whim
a first class of just one of him, he mused,
and wandered, with his baggage ticket, off.
He never boarded. Whether he confused
the embarkation hour with fictive tryst,
or, cabined, feared we'd know him false as toff,
our guess, who, from taffrail, was lost in his own mist.

An Afternoon's Reflection

Peter Parasol picnicked plumly placid.
All creation spread plumped out from Here,
Possible's Pumping House. Nothing rancid
poured from Peter's supple supposing, paired
to each object of what perceptibly is.
There's no rot imagined, for rot isn't
imagined by who posits perfect This.
A mind how comely still's a mind proves schizent:
Voici! the proofly picture; voila! the stone
to kick at. Peter, languid, didn't kick,
but vagaried a universe his own,
with every perfect Form the one he'd pick,
but for the abject fact the real'd dispose
to unname all its bits writ verse or prose.

*

If Peter sacked the tower for the lax,
and pulled a gold-shot arras down for robe,
so passed out to the parapet to tax,
usurper, far as he made out the globe,

if Peter picked a hamper up to gauge
how weighty proved the chicken from the eggs,
for crisp or devilled, what begins on page
must answer a real which its question begs,

if Peter piped a singing of the sea
or placed guitar or jar or blackbird where
their echoes into silences sang me,
though nowly Pete's less palpable than air,

how promptly paid, the premium to find
such evidence of Peter in my mind.

A Not Quite Unconsidered Prayer

On those days I can digest Stevens, the all
differs, and, though seen gobbets, is whole.
The light defers to a presence making fool
of obtuse me on those, craw-stuck, I can't,
when light lies on, glacé, and, as I want,
tantalizes appetite by simple dint
of almost.

            But a noon of Wally on the page,
when words come prised out pearly whorls, oblige
a peasant awe, and his high table gauge
what's realer after, now I've picked a meal
down on and into, laughing I could steal
such fire as I guzzle harmless, essence full:

a week of those before the roses close,
before cold, star-bit empty eats the clues.

Mike Feeds the Pigs

C'mon, c'mon! Mike's gonna feed the pigs!

Out from the party, down the garden path,
laughing, talking, holding beers and cigs,
toward that sort of joke we held in faith,
a Mike production, something girls and boys
of th'academic persuasion'd feel sorry to miss,
from their little cubicles, sans real-time joys,
the like we had! Mike's feeding of, ah, bliss!
the pigs.
   Held up, behold!
         the Penguin *Farm*,
Euchoiros!
    that good Sri Lankan bloke tore
the spine, and riffled out to sow and boar
the proof that we were greater!
        What, then, the harm,
that great, unthinking bulks of pigs could bless
with squealish tales, his,
       and our,
         swinishness?

The Demon

The colonel thought example might be made,
and ordered that the orderlies attend.
Desertion must regret, and to that end,
the lads must know whom that trussed lad betrayed.

A brother, too, in the same regiment.
Such witness would assure no sapper tried
to laugh it off or make out someone lied.
A brother'ld act to see the name repent.

The colonel, pleased, went down to the parade.
Decision braces so a man's resolve.
He'd give the nod to choice the major made
for names to make a squad, and he'ld absolve
by talking up the blank, just one, apart
from bullets that'd smash the sad boy's heart.

Mimesis' Nemesis ...

Who weeps for Fafnir, dead these thousands-year?
A dragon should be mourned, who has been slain,
a dragon who will never fly again,
a wyrm whom someone surely found once dear.
Well, fuck, eh? Yet the sun still shines, the rain
still falls. Like Fafnir, for whom none else cries
his golden scales, the emeralds his eyes.
So, fuck, eh? Surely dragon grief's inane,
that is, grief for a dragon, not the grief
we all cry for ourselves as selfish pricks.
Some stupid, mortal man, for stupid kicks,
hacked out a dragon's throat. Beyond belief,
eh, fuck? I haven't seen a dragon now,
well, years, and who'd give one anyhow.

and a Peek through the Other End of the Telescope

The Yellow Emperor outstrode the Sun
across his land-skin, marked each detail hung
within his golden, governmental eyes.
His Lady Leizu wove a body veil
more intimate than kisses from the sighs
of silk, so none, regarding him, could fail
to witness. He, to show his love, from dung
of dragons made for Mistress of the Han
the charms for being human, that prevail
today, though so fewer can recognize
the characters or clots they're written in.

And, from his ancient death, he lives again
forever. Stories east of Eden spin
his stuff from misty stories human size!

The glaze on pot once locked the potter's gaze
to mirrored moon. Atop transparent celadon,
centuries later, as well where mine's gone,
in this dark room, in this dark house, the phase
full thru windows and floor-spilt, a-craze
as fitted boards sea-sheened my faith walks on.
Twelve hundred years this bowl has been,
a thingness dumb through nights, and wordless days.

Except its curve confirm to hand that will
first drew it up from what spun on the wheel,
racked it, let it dry, and fired it, held it
to the sky, swirled it through the tub of glaze,
and fired it again, that flux weld it
to this world, and ripple moon into my gaze.

Cowboy Songs

Greed and Want

I guess I'll go hunt me a banker, two buttons and ox
ford cloth, tie. The bail-out has made me so
hanker to red dot a head in my eye.

For Cuban cigars are embargoed to those who can't
lever the cash to pick up a product black-cargoed
and watch the worth lengthen to ash.
                                    I b'lieve
I'll just make it a junket to find out addresses for fun,
one knoll sloped enough for a market correction
by God and by gun.
                      I can't get a licence to hedge
funds, but Jesus said I can bear arms. So I think
I'll go stalk me those someones who've been the real
source of my harms.
                      House is gone, kids, missus.
Truck's only mine while I run. I'll get no bonus.
A banker would fill up the freezer, if I had one.

10-Point Bucks

Jamie Dimon JP Morgan Chase
Lloyd C. Blankfein Goldman Sachs
Kenneth D. Lewis Bank of America
Richard Davis U.S. Bancorp
John J. Mack Morgan Stanley
Ken Thompson Wachovia Stanley O'Neal
Merrill Lynch & Co. Chuck Prince
and Vikram S. Pandit Citigroup

Savage Model 110 Elcan
DigitalHunter DayNight, Ruger
Model 77 Aimpoint 9000
SC MOA Red Dot Marlin
Model 366 Burris Full Field
II Tactical with Ballistic Plex Reticle.

At the Throat

So many murders never stop their hearts.
Are never murders but the wishing dead.
So many knives are bought and never used
(no matter that a penny's paid for gift)
the way they dreamed as ingots in the forge.
The tang to heel to run of blade, yes, chop
or peel or flense as use can fit the hand,
but cut to sever pulse that spurts the blood?
So few, the knife rings out as gong along
its edgy steel thrown down, its drinking song,
its lovely, brutal throating of a rage
into an after-panic, when the knife
can say it never really cared, if you

touch the wholeness of your skin, and breathe.

The Expectation

From Stevens' article of faith: The the.

depends that gist of knife: a murder means,
and all impatience is the hone you lick
across the stone toward fantasied
potential, noumenon! Of course, you're meat-
aphor! Who better worth? The truth, she was
Marilyn who had to tuck up her failed
breasts, her puckering ass, her slack thighs.

You didn't know Gerry Ferguson laughed
at you? A chimney Hitler, my wife called him
behind his death, because he, short, *smoked*,
and she keeps mistaking Adolf's historical height.

Go away into a wild then, with a cloth the length of your outstretched
arms, one sharp blade and perhaps your dead grandfather's garden boots.

A Country Drive

My name has buggered off. It left a note
about its reasons (or excuses), stuff
I'd thought we'd dealt with long before it wrote
to tell which tired whys had made enough.
It didn't like adoption, didn't care
that I had grubbed our way to muddle crass,
decollared all my shirts so they'd not share
a blue with white. *You blow it out your ass!*
it sez right here, as though I never gave
the very things it wanted, bits before
and after of respect, what names crave
to make them more than words, let them ignore
their letterless beginnings, till a grave
needs marking. Anonymous, now, to my core.

*

If I imagine Dublin (for I must,
a son of Oirish son who's never seen
the storied clichés filmed ancestral green,
the troubles, the romance, that Oirish lust
sublimed to boozy sentiment, the trust
I'm being lied to, so complete that mean
just doesn't play a part) ah! Dublin! clean
as fairy dust, and folks all uppercrust!

Not that my Ma, half-French, half half-breed, spoke
in glowing terms of that far-fabled town,
since Da took to another woman's bed,
and left her with three boy-sized mouths, a joke
she never got the humour of. She'd frown
at Dublin's mention, wish its people dead!

Ah, Dublin! How I wish I had a tale
so freighted with a cat-lick poverty
that I could brag a snot-green sea not fail
to keep its seabed from a yet-to-be.

Then maybe boy who grew to write this myth
would find himself admired by citizens
as take the Liffey chronic, scented with
the treated or untreated muck of tens
of thousands Oirishkind! I'd like to meet
the wonder in their stories! Rather I'm
as good as bastard, blessed with unctuous deceit
of Oirishness by a scrammed father's crime.

So Dublin has to wait for Air Miles points.
I'm not a lad the Liffey's sludge anoints.

*

I could have loved my father. Might have tried
to tie my shoes the way he wanted. Dad
was what I needed, one whose sweat just dried
instead of dripping from his nose, who'd add
some reason to my life, and last beyond
this moment from a past, in which a drip
would splot on toe. A boy'd not form a bond
with one who sweated so. I'd sooner skip
the next ten years, and the second best
of stepfather whose name is nonetheless
the one I sign to cheques, who to my breast
I never took, dead now, so what's to miss?

My wife, at forty-nine, thinks me a goof,
to let that kid within look for its proof.
'O, Lard, pesarve us!' Grandma, pickling cukes,
cried out.
              That,
                    later,
                          outside Budapest,
I witnessed hot lard poured in a crock
on fried chops to keep the meat the winter,

and I invoked my Gran, who was that fall
to die at ninety-four, and who'd cried out
on hearing how I wanted so my father.
Both dead these years. Perhaps it's for the best.

Oh, I have brothers, sisters, half, I know,
from tracing how he disappeared, and I
would kiss them Oirish, love them till I'm gone.
But I'm the one, in finding them, who's wrong.
No heads for verse, but cattle-raising brawn.
So rough, these lines, they'd never say were song.

*

But theirs a name was settled on before
the first of them was suckled. On the box
at drive-end, there it was, and nothing more
was what I took away.
                        The starling flocks
swirled up from staves of wires, fermatal trees;
the rain began to pucker dust beside
the road that splotted dark, the dark a tease
of sweat-drip on toe-leather, and untried,
the drive, the door, the cooking smells, the eyes

which might be wary as my hope that went
to find another name, by luck,
                                or find
it needed none to be the many I's
that make up me. And what can I resent?

He helped them tie their boots. He was their kind.

Our True History

The bread of Shoah falls unleavened ash.
Geronimo waits hunkered by the fire.
A killing, Mister Colt has made, in cash!
The flames spark up the manna of desire.

Israelis learn their fascism from need.
The Prophet hefts three stones to bleed a wife.
Elected popes sire bastards to the creed.
Surviving sons have dreamed a lifetime knife.

But cat must pounce galvanic on the vole.
But hawk must lurk on snag-top for the finch.
But spruce must snap in wind and by its fall
cripple its young that must outgrow that pinch.

Geronimo chews Shoah in his grief.
All Colt's bastard murders shout belief.

*

My mother's siblings wanted much denied.
A photo of her with her brother, Bill,
both knobby-kneedly thin, a-squint in sun,
and chewing bread that had some sugar spread,
is blurred as though their souls, already snatched
into the stranger's one-eyed box, had lied
as somethings worth the saving.
                                        Stop.
                                                The still
ongoing of that moment. See the son
and daughter of some *stetl* farmer. Each head
about to be shorn. Behind them, wire, matched
to the blur of scrub. *Arbeit Macht Frei*
near writ in the trees' halo. But the snag's
the click's too past. The sugared bread's awry,
the frock she wore torn cleaning rags.

Adorable li'l injuns, almost white,
but best not know how they might spend their night,
and best not know how girl and boy were made,
or if their sire were drunk, or dam afraid.

The mirror's depth is generations. Cheek,
ear angle, hair curl, eye
a-glint and fully who, singular,
                              deny
nothing of ones five deep, unique
each, but masked on that glass, the who unknown.

My blood, my tribe, my own.
                              I have a stone
from the Dordogne, long before the trader
had his counter, preacher, pulpit, master, chain.
And in its flinty heart it does remember
hand. Hand. In the mirror. Once again.

    *

Geronimo has ghosts that seemed to've favoured
in portraits, Mr. Sharps,
                              Misters Colt
and Remington brand loyalties that seem to've wavered
throughout the burning fervour of revolt.

His soul was taken, pinch by bit. Celan
cried blonde and dark against the ash, and no
thing, no thing, no. The river ran
in anguish through his dreams. What can we know?

By mornings I regard the mirror face
and it's no thicker than a pane of glass,
though line and ridge and fold of it retrace
such hungers, dreads and laughters of the pasts,

I ask what bits of egg and sperm are me,
and which were haunted from the first with 'Be!'

Much later, when the world had changed, and ifs
became the so's, her Sears likeness, and she,
as handsome as a background drawing Troy,
this Helen, mother of my sins and gifts!

We all adore our mothers. Or we say.
But in that core (the Heart!), we can't agree
if small disgusts outweigh the good that drifts
from bullshit and accretes to *Mother*. See
the fool with strings attached!? Does this annoy
your sense of justice?! Would you
                                     last the shifts
to keep that corpse alive, the counted lifts,
on *three*, and bed-sored, smelly limpness free,
we somehow know, of all decision,
                                     boy?
Relent. The end is nearer. And is me.

*

Geronimo is just a figure, called
for courage out the fuselage's not,
down atmosphere too quick to breathe and *thunk*
as pulls on boot-soles. The taking of the heart
as prize, the eating of it raw, the name
of fiercest savage the West has ever shrunk
to legend, here is courage. The girl I balled
to motherhood, hauled into my story by lust,
as echoless as breath in falling, silk
or death, either white in blossoming. Trust
the 'chute, its cordage, pulls. And trust the milk
from breast of mom or cow, or even goat.

Geronimo is dead, and all his wives.
But so is Brigham Young. Though Utah thrives.

Such Plea as Only Living Makes

Ah, yes, I'm here, if you're out there, God.
The itch in your sock, the nothing, once you look.
This conversation's so one-sided, so odd,
a grown man talking to himself as took
a lone walk on a beach where the tumble's shook
from dawn's gold foil these rattling hold-fasts
in the draw-back, presumption something lasts
when nothing does. You, 'god', leave me forsook.

Oh, be there, be there, be there. As gull that pecks
the eyes out of a skull, be there, mine!
I need. I want. I think I want. I am
this desperation on this beach who lacks
another. It's wind's churned up this flush of brine.
And I am here alone. I am. I am.

The Exile Weds His Island

This knowable universe, under this night sky,
that, if I had a soul and it were swimmer,
would be the plunge pool where the presumer
with soulless mind hesitate before it deny
as small coincidence the ever-why
of depth,
            this Jurassic flow of rock-grammar,
lip of my leap, and gulf the tic of stammer
between each star, hard time-fall high,

my island no more mine than I can own
the air my breath, the what cooled it to stone,
wind without a sea that from this cliff
makes just this possibility from if,

a faithlessness the leap before I know
which which these present waves might, timely, show.

The Island Knows Its Own

For M.L.C.

She's willingly convinced that dogs have souls,
as good as, if not better, than most men's.
The locals laugh, who've chased among the swells
the sober whales in drunken boats to cleanse
their own god-hauntings, but despite their spells
of feigned superiority, doggedly she minds
her own, and meets their morning-after scowls
with no presumption she must try amends.

If some men drink, and then, because they can,
harass great beasts by boat, if some put down
a dog because it needs, or some pretend
they know life better, and their laughter frown
that she persists, what might they understand
of dog-healed love, of whale-back glisten?

For H., on His Becoming My Daughter's Husband

Of course, I doubted. Who were you to bear
her complicated living, colicked lump
of tiger burning dream, as though the air
itself were raiment, bare and kicking plump
on changing table? Who were you to take
into the cordage of his heart the knot
she tied me into? Stranger, would you make
her pleased her other'd be so kinned in thought?

But all of love is giving. Know your place
(and, yes, you are that young, for I've grown old
and care a moment, calling scent and face
to hope you *are* that how her cord unfold)

awakes, my other son, to find no fright
if tiger's grass-hid in your very sight.

Discursion

For R. L.

The sentence doesn't feel the snip of line
coming, has nothing in its sprawl decides,
'Here's where a joint carves!' Its periods dine
more leisurely at thought; a clause confides
a subplot; phrases chat their head-words up;
while power-gathered, time-haunted verbs
work out to tendrils and make things stop.

But lines count out their integers like barbs,
the sharp held in the soft. They convolute,
do lines, obsess the text to fit the rhyme;
they dream and chant, and by their absolute,
can make of simple prose a petty crime.

Though lines pretend they never would offend,
no honest sentence ends itself with 'and'.

The wordlessness of sun on sea resigns
me to the echolessly sounding surf,
whose ragged bits, thrown up, are holy scurf
of weed and wood in almost made designs,
a drying furthest line the tide defines.

If such an animal event is birth,
dumb and all at once, each pebble's worth
a wet beauty babble first refines,
as wave-slur up the sand begins a sense
no lexicon can own;
                                        its word is whole,
and said, and said, and said;
                                                                as sky's immense,
translucent vowel, breathing, might console
the thoughtfulness of death with now's full tense,

reciting from its shoreward roll each scroll.

The Demon at the Solstice

The war is eating men again. The news
gets quite excited, telling sorties, bombs
by roadsides, coffins on the tarmac. Qualms
can't govern us at times like this. We choose
to listen or we flip the switch, amuse
ourselves some different way. If our palms
prick sweaty while we're trapped in listening, calm's

the soundtrack next station. We can refuse.

But here, the wind's long vowels past my ears
report Orion's red-patched shoulder, far
as death, and peepsight heaven's titan gears
rend new this longest night. There's war
inside. Though twilight balms the west, my fears

see something brutal in that nightward star.

A Vote for Mrs. Palm

That fragrance, fat, the volatiles of sweat,
mine, stain my pillows as I make my bed,
to lie tonight so weary in. Women
don't like talk of this, or dried yellow
on the seat's underlip, how'd it get
there, did you put it up? but I instead
who clean alone and make my bed, bordello
wondering at times, for Al knew when
his dollar lasted longest, 'Whorehouse, son!'

But I have ever been a wholesome fellow,
not paying outright for it, though I pay.
And pay. And pay. And pay. And pay, and pay.
And here I am alone, while latest she
is off and spends what earnings, without me.

Divisions of Labour

The twigs beneath the apple tree were downed
by storm that froze them in. Not many'd see,
in these ungiving times, calamity
that robs who needs of scabby fruit. A frowned
annoyance if I'd point them out, a ground
for judging me a fool, when patently
a curve of fender, drape of coat agree
much more with what has value, what is sound.

With luck, none hear the twilit deer that come
and teeter hindstood craning for sweet knobs
of winter wizen; none observe, in numb
and dazzled noon, a peck of blue jays mobs
the harsh-etched branches, tree itself stay dumb
to who brag cloth and steel and wealth-tied jobs.

The colder it gets, the harder the stars shine.
Great pressure creates diamonds, stones
than which nothing is harder, not will, not bones,
not love. Once I thought such softness mine
as daughters are supposed to have. Time
does what it does, and next thing, love's ruins,
a daughter's long distance, beyond the moon's
far side. It's not wrong, it's not a crime,
it's just love that sometimes goes awry,
and daughters go away and never say
whatever made them go, like stars are hard
and cut so perfectly, they cannot lie,
while, untogether, dads and daughters may.
Nor ask who cared, unstinted and unmarred.

For Inie Platenius,
Who Felt She Had to Kill a Rooster

Confusion's the prerequisite for grace.
The moment that the sparrow on the block
(where rooster, warm and bleeding, took his knock
for eating costly feed and giving chase
to layers when the lead beak's not in place)
cocks her head to ask your anger, shock
of recognizing self makes chance to mock
the fiend who grasps the anger you'd embrace.

So why be bothered raising chickens if
the purest agent of their killing's rage?
The plucking of that rooster, growing stiff
now on the snow, can't be enough a wage
for chicken-wiring pens. The fiend will sniff,
'Just who is on the inside of the cage?'

The Pomegranate

So often I've told you, 'Here's the fruit of Dis,'
yet you eat one so neatly, hardly Death
could wait for you to finish. Though each breath
bring you the closer, lips stained from the kiss
of juice prepare for black horses the abyss
lets up to race, hear them? you pick the pith
away from kernels, a caul obscuring myth
as though a future'd let you reminisce.

But no, the daily Lethe flows so strong,
it carries off this moment. We forget
so much, the story, and the story's needs,
the weight, by which the story's right or wrong,
lets anchor in the current what regret
sticks changeless for the sake of four small seeds.

Metempsycanine

I need to tell you that my dog will die.
That death is certainly a commonplace,
but dogs? My dog? A dog is without grace
and soulless, will not be redeemed. Though I,
I'd sooner darkness with my dog than try
the path into the light alone. A pace
a time, one hand outstretched, and one to place
her here beside. And what do I defy?
The master of the afterlife? The face
caught in the kerchief? There's someone I disgrace?
My dog? She farts, she sheds; when she wants out,
she wakes me in the night. The dark is what
you fear, but with a dog beside you, nought
can harm you, not Christ nor Dis, nor life's trace.

Spiegel im Spiegel

Is your mirror constant as your seeing
day by day no change at all slip down
its deeping well until its doubled being
break the self seen? Mine cracks my frown.
The dog's muzzle grizzles and meat, I sprout
nose hairs to a suffocation dreamt
by the small-pored boy hiding out
in my breath's Golden Age. The glass can tempt
by its hard surface you to seem frozen
to that you whose shock on meeting the child
some years later knows the face chosen
by absent sister for you, arrival's wild
rechancing of concourse, a voice booms in the echo
saying your name as she did, the eyes, so.

Some Assembly

Inertial in our words, that, unlike us,
remember, weighs, corporeal, the real.
Since Aristotle guessed our senses feel
first conviction, the photons' trick, crests

pushing coherence above the sensors' setting,
you fell for, this, to you, disembodied voice
is past process that sank down the energy well
and washed out the other end fertile. Insert slot A.

When we solve Tourette's, we'll find it's limbic thresholds
too involved in language. 'Fuck!' tells
that sex shocks this tongue, but universal
monsters startle always to 'Shit!', the potential's

such. How much nothing do the sensors need?
How insubstantial, word? Into tab B.

The Martyrdom of Claus:
Too Late, the Resistance

Sebastian has his arrows, for the saint's
alive in prayerful faints. That Lucy's eyes
are plattered and regrown, both, denies
the contradiction's edge, a-prying. Complaints
go up the ladder to some boss who paints
a tempting picture, with its snakes and lies
and fallen feinters, and so many pies,
the sky's a mansion full, without restraints.

It's not we want distrust. The boss's face
need not be sweet as queen's, and stamped on coins.
But we would keep our fancies from disgrace,
our arrow-eyed hopes where the heart joins.

It's not we'll gainsay suffering or laws.
But we refuse to nail up Santa Claus.

Dead Offices

How Things Work

The policy was, dogs were not allowed.
Dogs must be tied outside but not near doors.
No smoking was permitted. All the floors
that led to bosses shone, those walls endowed
with portraits and brass plaques. The halls that followed
to cellars where the work was done by Igors ...,
well, you get the point.
                              Are all whores
ladies? The ladies even paid? Hallowed
into headhood, do the ladies know their tasks
are useless, hence no cause for work? Harmless
scourers, shiers from any eminence,
do the ladies' maids ever don the masks
to hide their twilit longings? Look at the needless
repetition of rat experiments!

Why You Must Make a Living

Dirty language rubbed hard on your soul:
a guard dog humping dangerous against.
Shoo it, shoot it, chase it back to links
rattling when it leaps. The metaphor's whole
thrust is to the too complaisant role
you've played to get the teat the world maintains
solely for you. The coalescing agonist
with whom you share this virtual space thinks
only thru these words. You are alone
under the streetlamp, the dog growls behind
his fence, your cities are dystopias,
the simple fill your countrysides, the night
you turn to is so ancient that its mind
pays little you no heed. It's witnessed species
fail to stone, has no care left for your plight.

Collegiality

You're OK, spud, but don't the others secrete
nacres of seeming centred on such specks?
Blame, guilt, regret: Who drinks, who beats
up whom, who hoards, who whores, who scoffs, despairs?
I'll not presume to show you how to read
again, but you gossip back, for you know secrets:
our piss marks the same tree.
                                        In there,
they slap backs of least incompetents,
raise effigies of most brutal, equally.

You've found you're in uncharted time alone.

And that I trust in you. Things I've done
you'll never know. History fractals sequelly,
a beach we wander between and catch a tone
of voice grinding to a polish the lustrous bone.

There's No I in Team

Come see the photo of D___d's face a-grin,
an imp as ever made work hell and lean
downstage right doing what a-bend
to box of paper, paper, papers and
the big boss looking bland, a bit
confused about his role, but cueing at
upstage centre, just in case he proves
front page. That caption says who loves
his work, does D___, or is it caption says
the room looks shabby, like too many days
have rendered round head shiny and the grey
be not just photo black and white. Oh, look!
The office mate who smokes a lot of dope,
exiting stage leftish, just to cope.

Payday

If you quit now, you'll never know. Some clichés
catch you, don't they? Rhythm. It's rhythm. You're mostly
a kid of hicks' kids come to the city
with no ancestral memory, no replays
allowing whiskers and tight braids their says
on stone boats and stove black, stares fiercely
anonymous from sepia. You relish you're uniquely
yours, poor moult. Beyond, Chance sashays.
An unfelt thread connects you as She whirls
thru too large dance steps. She keeps her crickets fed
as She wishes in her well-dreamt world,
unheeding while you thrash against the skirls
She jigs to, by guess past questions deified,
She jerks you back until you're dry and curled.

On-the-Job Training

'You and I, who are we?' asks
the pessimistic officemate, convinced
at least I'm useless. 'A private, harmless vice,'
she's judged, my love, these words. The dead's tasks
include showing the dead's children what saps
their energy so's proving ongoing I's –
the soul above, just back of, the right eye's
socket they can't unlock for fumbling with the hasps.

But have you never once felt welcome here?
Has never thunder from the well of night
brought you gasping upright? Is something there?
Instils your peace, your terror? I choose to bear,
or so I fool me, mystery, but your fright,
arm out, thrashing darkness, swirls up my fear.

A Cheap Parting Shot

D___, if I knew where sank your grave, I'd hire
a thug to piss on it. To picture mire
by winter pressing down on your decay
proves tenuous revenge, since comes the day
I'll be in that same fix. I'd rather got
a shot when you were hot against your gripes,
the towel-heads, the artsy-fartsy, me.
I tried to have collegiality,
but you kept ragging on about the snot
factor, until, in a gritty stairwell, your snipes
stopped a student's ascending. My third
year charge. A bit of a crush, there.
And you embarrassed us by what she heard,
the sour, the rotting enmity you'd bear.

Separation Anxiety

So, S___, really, what a waste of time!
you saying mostly things you didn't mean,
me meaning just those things I wouldn't say.
So cute, oh, right, that you're the mother hen?
and I an integer of brood? No, I'm
gone and glad, and you can be cliché
The Man, and take the credit, till the Boss
decides the place can last beyond your loss.

And no one will remember, ten years out
when fresher faces fill the halls, and you
a name a careless fondness drops like waste
just near enough the bin to almost count,
that leaving was for me a blithesome haste,
the axe, the hen, the brooding, quit and through.

All This, and Benefits, Too

The not-yet-exile'd talked no godlessness,
but made wise with cracks that if recorded
would delete him.
         They'd show up unknocking, heedless
of client traffic, transcribed voice as witness
and haul him off, swiftly and justly rewarded.

The exile-to-be preferred a Gauguin, the only
documents some purchase contracts, homely
reminders that greed buys those girls comely
enough to fuck for the cost of a new frock.

There are some guys desert to make their luck.
The exile-elect avoided hot oil
and fiery arrows out on the battlement
by holding down a desk job. Any turmoil
crossing its surface was from Manapement.

The Martyrdom of Claus: The Gritty Side Revealed

The nature of belief is such that lies
get told to help the job along,

>   so great
>   a work that surely getting born's surprise,
>   hello, it's life, you are, poor child, now hate
>   your parents who did this to you, is more
>   a task,

and silly that you ask, 'A God?'
when all the churches don't know dick, but score
their right to tithe by politics. Give the nod
to good, and what of evil?

>   Balance Klaas
>   with farmhand, vulgar, brutish, gripping switch
>   to beat the naughty backsides, and the brass
>   to use it. Nether echo, Satan's itch.
>   Knecht Ruprecht's version gives that stooge
>   a stance behind, left-neck-craned, huge.

Game Theory

Your wedding gift to me
was so much guilt, I'd never
pay you back the ovens' worth.
The cattle cars on sidings. Sour
of earth. Sure, every rose
I brought you had to wilt.
But any home I rented,
bought or built would burn
the threshold moment,
bunk or berth but nowise bed
in night's so narrow girth,
slats and ticking on which
dark'd been spilt.

If every time your eyes
reflected skulls, if in
that crook where shoulder
met the neck a whiff
of Zyklon B, if ashy culls
snowed down your small
history, the wreck a marriage was
was hard forespoke,
an antihistory, denying folk.

The fear that drives us thru the night
to three
>   when restlessness will see
the numbers
>   clock
by mindless counting
>   argues

there's no talk takes back
the truth we're here,

>   the monster's free
and stalks the pulse a-tick
in temple, spree of panic's
breathing tight, the heart must knock
on heaven's gate, or hell's,
and nothing baulk at
any claim that nothing's not,

while we the fear has driven
(and, good bitch, reclines
alert to wait her master)
>   we're alert
as well for stair-squeak,
wind-creak, oblique signs
of that approach, that absence
pulling hurt out from its ragged,
too commodious sleeves,
to eat its blank through
all a heart believes.

The Source of the Nightmare

The fly's no more insistent
than am I. He'd rather stay
where I would shoo away.
He wears his shape as I wear mine,
by day exactly fly or manly,
but the tie to flesh in darkness
differs. Bulk persists as me,
but buzzing stops, or, rather,
dies in corners where the shadows
trick my eyes. And shadow
will not shoo. Such dark insists.

Beelzebub's a truly ancient name
that has no need of friendship
or for fame. So as I ready teeth
and face for bed, I'll just pretend
I know what buzzing said
gives all the scope to what
I shouldn't keep pretending
as I fall through doubt to sleep.

The Demon, for What It Is

The colonel had been buggered at his school.
That is, his arms were held, his drawers pulled down,
and several penises pushed in. The stool
thereon smelled shamefully his own.

Became the terror of the younger forms.
Took care to slap their plumpish bums to pink.
And helped himself, as head-boy, in the dorms.
Yes, power's learned as easily as ink.

Young suckling pigs, the colonel called them, long
before the army seemed the life. The war
was just the thing to prove oneself among
one's fellows, and stand worthy before the corps.

If once the whole endeavour seemed a boast …

a slack of body knotted to a post.

Late that's too late takes us to the rack, and
sumps from sleep a thickly earthy serum
animating dreams. We're forced to stare 'em
down, these underlidded visions, fecund

false prophecies, at our own peril wakened,
taking up our lives before we hear 'em
say the very words we'd use, but barren
purposed, with no meaning we'd've reckoned.

Golems decked in private natures, trekking
in our shoes an edgeless desert seasoned
only searing, dust-spermed devils egging
on our brutish urges to be reasoned
later, day, as blame, our follies begging
shrouds or questions, any hope that frees, and….

Speechless

At Baba Kot, they bury girls alive.
They shoot them first, to cut down on complaints.
If others try to intervene, say, aunts,
they shove those in as well. So there are five
as ditch-fill in the desert. That outward drive,
Abdul Sattar Umrani ranted cunts
don't get to choose. The elders know their wants
are frivolous. Baluchi girls must thrive
as owned by menfolk, says the book as read.
One reads, 'Thou shalt not suffer a witch to live.'
So Christians took them off by cartloads, gave
them screaming to the flames, those women led
headstrong to dissent. Girls bleed
but they are breathing as the shovels.... I've....

An Autumnal Question

Is *how* as big as *why*? My brother says,
'the nearer the end of the roll, the faster it goes.'
Because time freezes, we trust memory knows
what really multiples make up, the mess
of many tidied to one useful guess
that works nine times out of ten. A dose
of hot cynicism in hard science does
make some sense, if only as foil. Unless

you confuse the way it all works out with reason,
there's no attraction in the chestnut's shine
as the spiky pod dies back from the hard
and immediately perceived loveliness.
Which hand would you like cut off? Simple word,
how, small, useful, too great a loss.

The Confession

From the story of first texts, none survive.
No willing witness from the student's tale.
I'm sorry. I made them up. I'll go to Hell
by scruple. Not one was ever so alive
but in your mind as you could give the time
if not much space. You know they only quelled
their fear to talk with you, as if you told
the chance their longing see their author defied.
Each one knew it's all semantics. Deified
in his head as he writes This, each knew you
be speculated. In his blank as he pauses,
all cease. The void inherits from no sin.
Metaphor claws thru the rotting for any who
nests in the narrow tunnels of his clauses.

The Marginal Note on the Confession

Between us, you and me, we've raised a handsome
cast: a he, a she, a dog, daughters,
son, all forms of me, and hints of winsome
You. Outside the circle, the poet ponders
this passage and picks his nose. His take is, win some,
lose some; time dictates a tale that maunders,
not caring if it spend, or keep on hand, some.
The poet isn't thinking what he oughter
count, so many are the world's wonders.

The poet acts as filter for the words;
he knows he clogs on choices. You and I
have brought each out of shadow as we read,
and understand thru practice the absurd's
too easy moral of no judgment, why
they stand, and must, to serve our thought as deed.

The Specifics

He'd tangled so reserve up in her chat,
he'd only the long silence when she'd gone.
Her young face clearer than the one the bone
had moaned thru at the end. 'Remember that,'
he told the empty kitchen where he sat
to leave the most of frozen meals alone.
Where there'd been irritation now was none
to snap one word for fifty, tit for tat.

He'd learn, or die as well. The pots could cook,
and so could he. His cussedness, she'd joked,
was what had made him strong. If he'd been wrong,
she would have told him, wouldn't she? She took,
he told the kitchen, what had best provoked
that strength to grudge, its bit, her laughter's song.

The Generational Specifics

She'd gathered sapsicles so he could taste, sun
clear, first frozen spring. The doctor's haste
for nothing. 'His heart's gone, missus.' Faced
the wall. The habits of her fingers spun
in nets of doing held her to the one
salvation in her day. Awaiting the waste
of darkness and his death, that heart had cased
the loss of her in silence till it was done.
A life made up of many small kindnesses,
like stones heaved to the margins from the plough,
redeemed her torment of many a small regret.
She's settled in so many wildernesses,
his body first, his mind, his shifting vow
through her to what the fields let him beget.

The Historical Specifics

The babe new dead in her dead arms, Christ's
passion spent in a scant hour, the work waste
his hands had wrested, blood, its scent and taste
flooded thru the bedclothes, through his rage, the grist's
succumbing to the mill. Unwilled in his wrists,
the blood pulsed to join hers, a haste
as sinful as her taking, wrong, no worst
be had, one wanting mouth, two dumb breasts.

Condemned by pride and poverty to be
midwinter's midwife midway on a road
from market town to wasted nowhere, he
after unbecame an ancestral note
in register, on tax roll, formed no node
along a root that framed features by rote.

The Speculative Specifics

Don't look at me that way. This tongue still does
contain him, in words you understand. Language
shares itself among a social species.
We need chat, we need cliché and adage
retracing flickers on mind's wall. Oz
houses childish ghosts each twinkling edge
of need. Words drew her, freely, to his cause.

At some point she and he must die as mothers'
fathers, fathers' mothers, and be the myth
of two out of all the world with all
the world inside to share. Only as others,
not blood bound, not gesture familiar, with
no blemish or mark, before whom you are small.

The Textual Specifics

She knew the looking back itself was salt:
the ramparts an impiety, secrets raped
by day in narrow streets. So well they aped
the guest embrace, but stole the foreign art,
enslaved the music. The sport down in the pit
was what, with shouts, they owned. Then she'd no fate
left her, on that crest, but tear-cured hate,
she guessed, and looked back, desperate as fault.

He beside her couldn't move her after,
for she was second wife and first a daughter.
Confused, the path god-obvious before
thru fields leached greed-briny, he swore
to her, it seemed a maze, yes, but he'd been,
and knew that every valley out was green.

The Apocalyptic Specifics

A past so distant that his people's ways
wandered hill ranges, first cousins, then strangers
sometimes hulloing, come to barter wares,

then sneaks, thieving cattle, making slaves
of wives, and ash of crops. You know what slays
the unweaned child remains so small distinction:

eyeglint, skinsmell, hairshade. The extinction
of the threat. In passes, the one who waves
and stands still probably won't harm a chance

to palaver and hear if the old words still hold,
but you never know what waits just over the crest.

Her tribe flared in storied fire to outlines
on the stones.
                    Don't stand his heart in vengeance.
Its flesh-unstitching flame spits on all bloodlines.

The Stupidity of Pretending Specifics Mean Anything

The radio on the first Sunday of the new
war I'm reminded words sent great distances
as wave energies increase my heartbeat. No,
you say, the tones of voice, the well-formed
enunciation of official spokespersons,
foolish narrator. But it's spring! it's spring! and the words
small rainfreshen up reddenwing twigs,
and the war greens upon Ur of the Chaldeas.

Reported is the morning's drama of the city's
people out searching for downed airmen along
the fabled river, and soldiers shooting pointedly
among the rushes. The sound artist comments
his sorrow for the little bits of silence.
The dead are called out. The cries anoint, indeed.

Rather That Demon We Know ...

Now we're all poor again, the war will start
sniffing around our kitchen steps. Now we've
squandered bread to feed the park flocks,
a feathered blood will stain the walks. We leave
a half-glass of wine before we depart
the garden for our evening, dawn it's gone.
Now our children are caught beyond our locks,
out in the open of selfishnesses, the war
will laugh as it ruffles their hair, will ask
where they live, smile as their eyes look far.
The war's in love with pi's infinite slices
from reason's grasping on and on. It circles
back through painful memories, skews the dice's
throw over our wanting what we always knew.

An Aside for the Sake of a Dog

The dog is sick, who has been friend, not best,
perhaps, but true; the dog is sick, and deadly
sick and will not bark at you, as you
sneak near to see she's sick, and doesn't care
to chew her snack, and may well die from this
attack, and then what will I do? O species
that will play on side the game so closely
fought, so intimate the food is shared,
so teammate, and so ought, against the rat
and stranger, that the stranger's fled, and rat
is caught, and rest's shared guarded while the kids
are sleeping in their great, big heads on little
bodies sprawled alive and whole and free, who
waking, won't think to thank the dog and me.

*

For Horus, was pole star the hole out
of His suffering world? Khufu can have the pain;
let him take it with him. What about
death, too, dragging behind? Again
and again, his life ours, he goes, or ought,
to make a place for us. I know my pen
is slower than fate's tug; still, it's caught
up: my dog, my best critic, she's gone.

The liniment. I called it love and you
snuffed so curious. I'm sorry. The tease tempted.
Here's that fatty snack denied, a few
futile for the way, your stare emptied.
Now's bushwalks lead where, as if I knew.
Go find a way, so follow may attempt it.

*

The stars are holes struck thru the bowl of night
that find the edge of all-consuming light
where what is each falls into nothing's might.
Above her bed, Meg's ceiling glows in dark
with stuck-on plastic stars that for her mark
familiar navigation to sleep's spark.
And deep where dream ignites the womb-made dread
that near first light kicks restless in her bed,
she'll rise to leave those landscapes of the dead.
There, Suki, snoring truly stunk beside,
can stir at her first stirring, and decide
how safely, in what scents, the dream can hide.

But then I woke, and all I've told you gone,
returned to past, thru runnels of the dawn.

    *

If all the dogs were to die and we had to rely
once more on wolves, oh, there'd be some gnashing of teeth.
If all the sheep were to slit their own throats, and bequeath
their pastures the unfed grass, oh, there'd be cries
of the cold. If the wheat were to rust from drought, and seethe
up chaff in the wind, if all the cattle's sighs
drive their milk to exile, and the crippled scythe
lie down with bones of sheep and dog, and breathe
dust to dullness, oh, then we'd avoid each other's
eyes, oh, then the streets would darken early,
the children run and hide from unbearable mothers,
and the least grinning fool among us turn surly.

Already thin wolves steal down from the stony hills,
and the grass will not rise for the white weight of skulls.)

The Agonist Bitches

Truth is, I've come from Hell, and can comment.
There is no memory there, where time's perfected.
It's not at all what many have conjectured.
Longing's no more needed there than moment.
Hell has no mansions for us, doesn't want
our kind intruding any more than we
would welcome rats within the mortal city,
hour-diseased, and costing Hell the rent.

Our price has been misplaced. We're no more useful
than a flea circus, in which the tricks and acts
are more imagined than witnessed by the crowd.
Hell knows it could collect us by the nooseful,
but can't be bothered. Who made the problem? asks
Hell. You, our idiot, laughing out loud?

*

I'm your honest liar, as foretold.
Listener, if I'd said one word
other, I'd have broken faith. I'm no
exemplar, benighting with time-tied tongue
a fashion in effigies. Boy and fool, I've stood
for the halt, dumb before the law, the crowd,
the threat, the true believer and her god,
for fear sipped her altar's changeling blood.

If you'll trust one who claims faith infests
stone, another blasphemer next you'd set
your hands on, hear:
                              You'll know the idol's gaze
best in sheer, high places. If you've borne
your favourite instrument, then close your eyes.

Dance to your playing ever wider out.

*

When, smug with vengeance, you pronounce on me
your fatwah, remember that cosmologists have recently
decided, in an infinite universe, each replication
of you is detailed down to zero. The amend
will be made, for the chances are endless these words hear
themselves spoken over and over in all their
combinations, even as alien tongues.

If I persist at all among the songs
of other worlds, and my love-urge know I share,
beyond this flesh, beyond all temporal fear,
in my beloved's answer that leads to no end,
a fate of ordinary complication,
let your proclamation kill me decently
as one who wanted only one be me.

*

Let's say you're not easily won over;
my critical regard should first be you
secreted from I fleshed on inner other
dumb words reframe each time new, and true
that intuition longs for circles, but your very
possessed transfinite point as squirrel at feeder
fattens, so crow later lunch on answer
road-flattened, too stark to be true, chemistry

whining feed me, rest me, warm me, fuck me,
and how to tell one version from s'm'other
each finite breath until, in no more, free
from you, I wrest the lost cause I argue
from stuff's doomed rote, deny your right,
and blind me mute, appealing to the night.

*

So. All these feet I've fit to the same shoe,
a size 14, 5E. I was hoping for
the Cinderella story told anew,
but its tired characters've been coping for
so long a time with mediocrity.
Contagious passions should try to eschew
(bless me!) an easy virulence. Most we
need's filled bellies and warm beds, but few
get even those. There's no use moping for
a better ending when the possibility
the hero's dead leaves me groping for
a plot, whispered as what secret odd
enough to put some trust in one whose terribly,
poor man!
                    unfolded fate *must* be god.

*

A meatless, saltless soup, this too thin gruel
I've boiled up for you from time's grasses,
endless to horizon. Breath seems cruel
to let being feed am to a bottomless
I, since breath'll withdraw its witness. I'll
pass. See, Breath-Serpent encompasses
the desert as temptation. I'm a fool
've wandered out, got turned around. My guesses
about which way's back've failed, all.

This hospitality's the best you'll do.
I've shared out equal portions, as I've done
with fellows rendered in the earthy stew
that feeds the grasses, at least until each one
become again the breath-delivered new.

The Martyrdom of Claus: The Final Solution

If *santa*'s 'holy', 'consecrated', 'blessed',
and *Klaus* is from Manhattan Dutch before
the British took the farms, before the mess
America got into with a war
that changes faces, kills the young, and lets
Republicans get richer, who'd ignore,
among the chicken colonels taking bets,
all little boys, if good, can train for gore
and only faint for needles, that the best
thing's to take no chances, track the whore
on NORAD, just in case, and leave the rest
to family TV.
        And Mom, abhor
violence, don't let your boys play guns. Instead,
boost poetry, and manners for the bed.

The Inherent Pessimism of Rapture

Would die in exile joyful not empty would dance
the last as borning the first dance breath
as light's passage dance too you beyond
before and after any corpse lacks
grace, falls, rots. Text took from
one who forced Herr Death to honour choice:
Schreib dich nicht zwischen die Welten, komm
auf gegen der Bedeutungen Vielfalt, vertrau
der Tränenspur und lerne leben. Scribe thoo
nought between the worlds, come of gauging
the bedatuming manifold, make true make true
the tear's spurt and learn living. A voice
in wilderness where to discover musky sweet
of hive sing dancing in the thorn-pricked meat.

*

What does it matter? How does it serve that we
have come this far, and here's night again,
a silent woman who hears her children lie
and, by her silence, asks them who's to blame?
Companion in the dark, I will confess
the words themselves are embers of deceit
that, fanned by exhaled time, assure us less,
yet will not close our sight till night's complete.
As, in her vacancy, we sit and listen
to distant cries and sniff twitches of smoke
from unclean fires, my fellow, know the war's
this moment only written in our scars

and that I've always loved you. When we spoke,
our words sparked out the stars across heaven.

*

Bring kid seethed in its mother's milk, bring clay-
footed idols, bring pillared salt that we
may taste its lips, bring out our dead to pay
the fiddler for the pyre, that history
'sno more than shambles dream, a snore away
from waking cataclysm to surge up, free
of what we want so important, to play
at odds again, and form from our debris
the next by which we are forgotten, all.
And Adonai so old He talks to dust,
and stirs it, spits in it, invents a fall
that sin, which just means guilt, owe as it must
the startle in the night, where stars, mad, recall
each anguish of our sleepless self-disgust.

Another Small Song for M.

I call to the small god of lost causes
whose name is Forgotten. Out of my despair
she folds this origamic rare
bird, as answer:
                           you, my other.
                                        Posits
a fellow exile, Ur-lover who rouses
the ancient garden in me. Since I can bear
nothing but my thanks to that realm where
the god I pause for, I hope, also pauses,
before turning back to her wall to feel the cracks
for what's slipped thru, I'll give for you, I swear
in this true-grailled moment, that excess
of my life I wouldn't, unless, use, the stacks
of otherwise alone dawns, their bare
golden needles at horizon's endlessness.

The Demon in the Market

The war has never left us, grafted on
the rootstocks of our lust. 'Be gone!' we shout,
but it just finds new ways to kill, devout
as all our longings. And where the lines are drawn,
it chews the faces into skulls. Has won,
so long as it continues. And will sprout,
among the young, balled braggarts, whom without
we're damned not to be. Even God was Son!

Old men, enrich yourselves that those who'd die,
get eaten by the dirt and be forgot!
I knew one once, and beautiful as Olaf
in the long ago, but so long's your cash can buy
a national conscience, he was earth fought
into itself. Laugh, you senators, laugh.

The Exile's Second-Last Fate

Rumours were, the exile'd died abroad.
One had him tumbled down a mineshaft; one,
and more likely, made the claim he'd trod
on native toes; one put him on a life-raft
hopeless at horizon. The exile, meanwhile,
awaited mail until the postmistress
took pity and slept with him. Her guile
caused grumbles for weeks; the locals' distress
coloured their shop manners. When he'd done
his small business among them, the exile went back
to his headland, closest that shore from whence he'd come.
He saw the far sun-glint would never lack
for making blindness, the foam-maze write out *none*,
the laughter of the surf enchant him dumb.

The Demon's Privilege

When God's squeezed out the gonads,
                              bigot's frauds,
mit uns, In ... Trust, In Telly Gent Design
er (jeez, the wonder! Jeez is short for...?) whine,
whine, whine, and bluster, harangue,
                              applauds,
well, no one but the soldier, it what plods
by orders, hoping Heaven asks no *mine*
about the following,
                    and rise up, just fine,
on Redemption Day, uncloyed by murder's odds.

The colonel never thought beyond the right.
The colonel never thought. No, not a brute,
he understood a napkin's uses, wiped
away what needed wiping, held no spite
for them as squeezed the triggers, Wipers not
withstanding, no matter wanting teas they griped.

The Fisherman, as I Explain to My Son, for Whom I Wrote This Book

So here was Scotty closed the door away
from his kids, sat on the bed's edge, Lord,
he said he said looking nowhere exactly,
the verse opened John something, the word
was truth. He said. He got up from his bed.
Son, we're not talking simple fishing men,
but truth. His life's words. He said his head
was clear. He went back out to his kids, then.

He took those pills just one a night, his choice,
and truth outgrew its need for bigger shoes
until they walked out on their own. His voice
now gentler for the bearing this old news.

Son, trust he knows his tale's telling's
not took as bread, nor set so sure as dwellings.

*

A fisherman's time's fishing, and, sure, he talks
fishing, proud of its gear. A writer's day
winches its hours over the sorting tray
and the pick's the preoccupation. Cod stocks,
sez writer, fell through overfishing, eh?
Words are slick as herring, sez boatman, his cash
from urchins for Japan. The rest's trash
fish splashed dead overboard. Stowaway
in the story, the writer checks his shrinking cache
of credibility, oh, the boatman caulks
the shell in which he risks the sea's epochs
to drag its depth darker than his moustache
just so the customer can have her wish,
the tale's comfort, the plate of fresh fish.

*

So there you are, beyond the chat my son
and I are having here with no clue who
is Scotty, onetime nexdoornayber knew
a large bag of nothin', told me one
cold afternoon, but fishin'. Married young
and had too many kids for far too few
markets after the war collapsed, so
there you are. Can you return undone
his cocky, stupid youth, he asks, and would
he choose different? Would he leave some herring
for the food chain? Would he see your daring
to meddle as leaning down from the bow wood
to which you're knotted, kiss his brow and lift
his worldly cares from conscious him, your gift?

Here near the margin of the sea, a field
Small islands bob thru the illusion that
the sea goes on beyond forever, caught
far only at those unknown edges yield
its utter end. Here sere the grasses, sealed
into their roots, awaiting what is sought
as well by the rock-mothered sand, by what
already from winter's harm is rose healed.

The red hips insist to eye, the brine
to nose, and under foot, the earth draws down
the sense of its witness. I, by standing here,
vouch for this moment its windfall gain mine,
and walking on, can ask no more, nor own
other than this, in living, anywhere.

Epilogue

In these branchings, chanceful reader, hangs
the rictus of my dream. The thong does wrench
tight my banter to that trust might cinch
the seem to datum, stats to fact, and song's
entangled stammer to such longing as brings
my scheme crashing down. It was only hunch
we shared the sea upon which I might launch
your thousand faces, make you the beetle's dung.

No news here, then, this suffering. If you
swat down these brinked bones to make room
for your ladder, mind the urge you fought in sleep
was beautiful to weeping. What's left to be true?
Climb up and pick the fruit. The birds' doom
is shared entire with you, and yours to keep.

Appendix 1: The Exile's Fate

The imperium, impatient to render the wealth
its priests said reserved itself in those eccentric
enough to blame and banish for the health,
they claimed, contradictorily, of the body politic,
brought the exile back, his skull his cell.
Crowded full. Each memento whole.

But exile, torn away from sticks and stones
he'd sorted from his beaches, barefoot, brown,
couldn't tell, of hosts or guards, ones
from others, nor had the pinching shoes to own.

The first claims were that his distraction'd mend,
but it grew clear he would deny the rule.
To kill him seemed too wasteful or too cruel,
so pardoned and returned him to his end.

Appendix 2: The Log Notes

As east measures out
colours' weight against
the bluing shadow falling
the height from stars to sky,
its clouds obscured as white
from dark in wind's entanglements,
this late into the death of night,
the maggot, light, eats
into formfulness those trails
which on slate enchalk the letters,
without haste or hate, risen written,
moving on as these, the slight
increments by which day
convinces the senses.

They are, poor filters,
all you've got against
your idle, spiteful mind,
and your defences, waking,
like any mammal's, before
you stretch, confused about
which threats are likely gains
from where, in sleep,
the darkness waited, watched.

Awaking, there's the pause
while you decide. Arising,
you make new with it your pact.
Your lover, it surrenders breath,
this fact a small kindness overlooked,
confided without expectation, since
you've defied it more than once
for what you thought it lacked
in showing tenderness.

Its patient tact waits
to know how you will next
divide between your selves
your will, then gives a way
as it proves able, gracefully
aside to your effort. Less
than your thanks, the more
your day weigh its counter
to each your act, elide the you
of you within its caring weight,
the greater you stand to
deliver world's delight.

When you were young,
it wasn't your, you swore,
but love's, confusion.
Now love snakes away
thru that ignored tangle
where the questions stray
to danger. If, all the dark,
the surf's roar affirmed
your sleeping rhythms,
did you dream, for those
in peril, any rescue?

Aware your cupboard's
down to mice turds,
you stare into dawn's
trappings with sore,
sure fear. Usage-condemned
love! If it hadn't been the waves,
your heart's blood would so have shook!
Where among the stormrung bells
did you abandon your tried and tired
charity the way you took?
Warm and chew your want.
What you have is your lesson.
Love thieved from need,
when you became the crook.

So what did piffling you
want to pilfer? A little time?
Some wealth? A bit of knowledge?
That shadow's intuition where
the snow-ledge overhangs the roof
falls in as rime? Some perfect sense
can't be talked about, though there seem
almost the words you'd use to abolish
fear (whose cart, time, you've ridden;
whose haulage by its one fare
has cost your entire lot).

Moments, it's your own face
proves the stranger. Imagine
an amalgam of words such that some
suggest others, and the mélange of doubt
and certainty that ambiguity can give
a conviction nothing happens
unless it's live, makes right
any little treasure you might grieve.

If you think love's some sort of thought control,
well, love's first lesson's reason's knackless.

While love does need to kill you
as slowly as possible (otherwise,

it can't successfully replicate
all its variables, won't match,

can't mutate when needful,
makes just function of the milk from nipple,

will die), look: love made birds from serpents.
What it makes each breath of you will solve

mindfulness or not. In you evolve love's lineages,
and each death love laments yours. Forgets

and remembers the intent directed it
before your knowing self makes fresh,

from old, old patterns, you as love,
your thinking as its thought, your will its servant.

This crease where your left earlobe joins your jaw-line,
something just under the skin your fingers return to,
a pore ingrown. Nothing you can see in that awkward
angle in the mirror, but your fingers know. They keep
straying to it when they're idle. Times
your fingers are busy, your mind, which seems as discrete
as your fingers, strays, and the sins outweigh your heart.
The balance tips. You can do nothing for it.
You can't stay busy every moment. You get tired.
Your mind gives up into fantasy; your fingers stiffen.
Times your sweetie craves some romance in a long
distance call, but it's about smelling and holding.
Some nights you want to walk well out past
the lights, to see if all the stars are shining.

This universe in a grain of sand
notion: perspective's odd.

Into the future, more often
than not, you're dead.

Defining bits'll soften
and fall off, part away,

be else. There'll come
that dawn your comrades

find no pulse, or, lucky corpse,
don't find you, whose peels

are about feeding humbler lives.
You will not stay breath, argue

breath, braid air's knot into
a mysterious name that alive

thought, so were, as egg
from within your mother's

birth, as sperm knit
out of finely sutured earth,

by which the dumb rock
confesses faith, and founds

its tellings in which faith you are,
defined, whole born, rock's avatar.

A boulder beach allows you gauge
what ant's perspective be along a sandy stretch

for, as you find your way, a sort of dance
emerges from deliberate balance, each stepfell slip.

You know it's barefoot chance has figured
from the ground this frame to fetch upright,

and glints off facets bright(en)trance
your concentration makes for every match

of arch to rockhump, glad of rolled pants' cuffs,
daring the day, the way you catch,

by lifting forth,

the falling back.

Your stance, two-legged, not six-,
tips to let you snatch as ant-haunted fate
the reflex was once among these
so large grains that lurch at touch.

Fog.
      Fingers twinge.
            Slug weather.
                  You'll live's
the pity
      and settle nothing for the fog's
flouncing up the hill
          and flings its veils
out to arms of spruce

but brings specs-bouncing sneezes
shooting tingles thru their needles.

Congeals just past jelly: thumb-long
slug oozes by by belly.

Pain's not alone the lot of bones.

The tub of virgin privy lime or salt's
damp rub over board set next
the tender greens of garden,

and fortune's slugs don't scream,
whose slime-slide's as well the dance's dream,
and means same as joints' aches
                or fog's climb.

Shining flood of highest tide!
is how joy this morning for no
straightforward reason splashes over
anxieties and aches
                              – a pause like dashes
in a lifelong sentence: your costs;
your tooth annoy the so mild
disappearance otherwise of body –

a moment's nudged wink
at a brink that flashes the out in,
the in out, as tho flesh is the only
lamp for the casting of joy's ray:

primeval awe-fullness of that peace
to a creature what knows it dies
is nothing you would have thought to ask for.

Nor the bitch, though she dozes without
any attention at all to how close your foot
is to her muzzle, knowing you've nothing
to teach her she's not already aware an answer

glosses.

You will misread, for you always do,
the small pauses wherein the larger words are fixed.

To answer you, the bitch makes a howl small
and voiced which sounds, she thinks, in fragments

for you to understand the whole she speaks from.
From mistakes the phrases flex back to some point

admitting, yes, hale and sound this dialogue, on
twisted lengths of immateriality the haul, phoneme

over phoneme, to the links of knot that make up
the net the meant does roil teeming in. You hear

she's talking thanks for the herring tin, her part
of your meal. Your smile is hers, and your affirmation,

fishy licks.

No matter the specifics
of the kindling coaxed
to catch the thin sticks
brought in from the cold,
at the first heat, ice squealing off,
the hissing out of wet, and settling down
to new bedded coals caught in the grate,
glowing, ever the same flame, the same
ancestral sacrament, begotten from tattered
plumage, the fresh phoenix you tame.

The woodstove's iron walls
hold in no blame as heart or
mind might. That freed, in there,
writhing thru the chemistries it bathes
so hot in, tells, beyond whatever sort
of sleep you'll get tonight for cold,

fitful, deep,
           the stories,
                      stared to true,
from where you came.

Deep in the wood you dream the dog kills
a fluttering, rustling death, beyond your sight
but in your hearing, scream cut short, the light
somehow empties, bright still but stills
along the leaf, until breath, still sure, fills
that void that opens on the fall thru insight
to a plunge eternal with the ammonite.

Some, you're told, come upright, yell-willed
and woaded from their sleeps, bring disasters
then on their houses. The bloodied-jawed dog's
returned empty-mouthed to you. Afters
can again bumble away into monologues

muffled by an edge of quilt.
                    Awoken,
the bitch watches alone, her dream forsaken.

A private weakness, you know life
no better and no worse.
Not at all. Because it's you.

Who's afraid of life!? Without a mirror,
you're not old. Your real age is now.
Does knowing more make up for thinking

slower? Have you seen the sexing of chicks?
Fast old hands thru the chirping batch.
Ever caught in a curtained gloom

those old hands pronounce the corpse brow?
Creased. Dark in the nails. Knobbed at the joints.

One ties you to your birthcord,
one counts your pulse, one snips an end,
a round of three-handed chance.

Ever hear, beyond your dream,
numbers, pitiless numbers, and wake,
your palms stretched out to darkness,
your reckoning heart still full of hungers?

The perfect life has no chores. Each act
belongs to each other, the vowed contract
of starting, by joy, the stooping for a sock
because you are the Picker-Up of Sox
and the cast-off vessel one one lovely foot
bounced in, the dog's nose-curious game
sharing sacrament in the affection of it.

The perfect life's truth has no fame for not
a gesture acts anywise false,
                                        as Noh you might
only've suspected unfolding, does,
the blessed timeless moment of the whole,
untelling the lie that Judy found in Oz,

and what of the pills made her so very sleepy,
no perfect poppied air you'd breathe as deeply.

Ascented by cuntrich sea, the dog
comes in, her stone buried in the stone-
strewn garden. If you'd been David's line,
in Palestine, you'd be no better rock-lobbing
wide-eyed desperation against some bully.

The dog rushed for it into the whine-cold
brine and arose from her waters perfumed
by bog-purified, stream-emptied tincture
of the tide's pasturage the sea claims its salt

remains.

A well-thrown stone against
sealed armour roars turbulent exhaust
up your street, BONG, right off
the turret before the gun fires!

Golgotha's yet a ground of stones.
Your error jumbled wave-glints,
Nazis, poles,

desires.

Your speaking fades into that hum that sinks
below awareness, where moss songs of living

breathe the silence past which desert distances
drum uncared tediums. Electrons are diving

that long fall to stasis, and your speaking thanks
with each automatic word their effort at divining

love's potencies from tender resistances,
each meal's embrace an urgency dividing

among the multitudes. Love surrenders;
love obeys its needful freedoms, avoiding

of the darkness the threats to you and all your words.
What you speak resounds the world's revealing

gestations of monologues, bones' endearments,
and the blind heart's mumbled way by feeling.

It's the unseen new moon
raises the tide over the ragged line
of wave-cast weed and casts the weed again,

an artifact you thought lasts in knowledge,
like tying knots, or hearing, above her, that close,
the small, almost terrified 'oh' or 'hah'

freed to your shared dark. Facts are notorious
for quarrelling all your ways and knacks
to simple repetitions, where the prompts quiver.

Your breath's in no way theory, and your fuddlement
accounted in the rhythms of your kind.

You've forgotten, too, how the many fit
inside you as secretion, that returning's meant
what's passed for love, or something close to it,

to allow you make some habit of your mind.

You know your lifelong exile hides in you,
placental other, invisible from birth.

While you sleep, it watches as the Shadow,
allowing your reprieve from Dark, as Death.

Look at the rhyme: obvious; unprovable.
Who in god's name, _____,
would fall for that dearth of wit?

Who'd make the claim such cowshit's true?
Monsanto, making rational the soil?

One good way to quiet fear's
to feed as its one dish the dirt.

At the first dull drowsing of the lids,
contentment's smile, infant whole
and uncorrupted, you need simply
imagine it will never waken,

and freeze it into time,
stopped unbroken.

The first snow sings Palestrina as it falls.
Not, of course, in the air of the house, after
the fridge has done its thing, and left this hush
that should be Palestrina. Then why do you cry?

There's no kyrie or credo to question you. The quiet
is a perfect mercy. How can you weep? All's
one as the snow with unvoiced patience forgives
the lawn it covers. Oh, weep then, since you must.

It's not you crying at all, not for or by
yourself. It's that ancient hesitation gives
out to weight and falls. You'll feel better
in a moment. You'll get up and put your boots away
and make a cup of tea and clean your nails,

and let those last wet leaves for now stay piles.

*

This fresh night's sea-girth's smear of haze
'sa nowhere stars' old lights not pass through,
that've long sphered out the fainter for you
to take in larging dark. When sun spent prize
of sailor-splendoured red to seal the day's
tales in their versions,
                              no, that's saying askew:
It misses what's here meant before you, new
now as now its ever lineage is.

Time spreads as well out. As the night
holdfasts that much stronger so it sieves
the more of myriad up high an arc,
the far sulphured glow blinds with light
a city's say-nothings with too-much lives
who'd jape fear, jostle noise in this dark.

*

Oh, yes, I'd live forever, should you ask.
As long as world might live, before the sun
balloon out red, and even dirt then mask
itself as dead. Your face forgotten. Gone.

I know I'd lose this family, these friends.
I'd know the geese by V's in sunset end.
And how the force called life might shape it kinds
prove quite beyond this language in this mind.

I'd know as witness, though I know I'd lose
a presence haunts me, not a ghost, a *this*,
an almost calling forth of why I'd choose
to be and be. And almost find your face
at each dumb awaking, and wonder, Where's
she, that one I loved, these blurring years?

*

The apple falling to its bruise,
the grasses drying from the root,
have told no wind to tell their news,
though their noises tense the night
into a now, this place, where mine
are absent, save for bitch and me,
who have no hope for word or sign
but the moon-encumbered sea.

That nothing present will deny
the apple rot, the grass lie down,
that bitch will die, and so will I,
none other witness that the moon
seems smaller once it's climbed that high,

and this night not yet done.

*

The knife-edge slice that downs the sea from sky
heals, this twilight, gauzed in a far fog.

Of the seven human questions, that the why's
the only gropes towards hope, for some prologue
to a perpetuity, makes evident the size
of small us on this balcony,
                                and though we brag
our own, the great house's elder tribes
are off unnoticed, near as surf, or far
enough that we confuse the white that scribes
that surface.
                For depth, if it hold whale,
                                        or star
later,
    so much of this moment we'll ever miss,
nor can see holy.
                Know me here.
                        If I kiss
your cheek, I never will betray you. This only.

For who, or what, or how, you know,
                                if solely.

You'll be OK, though you lose it all. Create
your consent. Some stares were intent as hawk's, some never
met your gaze. Your most unjust temptation's
been love's by which you close, repeat in them,

all body, each many. They know your scent and wait
to find you where you stripe dry grass screening
savannah, beyond. Look, terrible, beautiful,
the eaters as their meat, angels such

as Rilke claimed he'd met! A. Hoggett's fiercely
truthful dance that love stuffed in his boots
with roots' strength removes all doubt that sheep

may safely graze. Dust, that'll do.

The loneliness rests, to your dismay. Their feast
will welcome you. You'll be OK.

Wayne Clifford was born in Toronto in 1944. He studied English at University College at the University of Toronto in the mid-sixties during which time he came to be associated with a small coterie of students that included Stan Bevington, Dennis Reid, Doris and Judith Cowan, and David Bolduc. While still an undergraduate Clifford won several Norma Epstein prizes and bursaries for his poetry and also one E.J. Pratt Award (1967) that he shared with Michael Ondaatje.

Stan Bevington had started his fledgling Coach House Press in 1964 and asked Clifford to acquire a few poetry manuscripts suitable for book production of an experimental sort. Wayne secured early work from George Bowering, Victor Coleman, bpNichol and Michael Ondaatje. Shortly thereafter, Clifford left Toronto to pursue graduate studies in creative writing at the University of Iowa.

Clifford began working at a small college in Kingston in 1969, and was involved in the Creative Writing Program and the Fine Arts Program, until both were discontinued in the 1980s. Clifford then began teaching remediation in language. He retired in June of 2004, first to Halifax, and then in 2007, to Grand Manan in the Bay of Fundy, where he built a house overlooking Whale Cove, and which he shares with his artist wife, M.J. Edwards.